JOHN STUART MILL was born in London in 1806. He received a remarkable education from his father, James Mill, the Scottish philosopher and historian of India; by the time he was fourteen he had studied Greek, classical literature, logic, political economy, history, literature and mathematics. In 1823 he and a group of young radicals formed the Utilitarian Society, and in 1824 the *Westminster Review* was established by Bentham and his followers, through which Mill and his Philosophic Radical associates expressed their political ideas. A devout Malthusian, he was arrested in 1824 for disseminating birth control literature in London. Then, in 1826, Mill went through a crisis which transformed his intellectual and emotional orientation: he began to be critical of the 'pure' world of rationalism at the heart of Utilitarianism, and to be concerned with the 'cultivation of the feelings'. In 1830, he met Harriet Taylor, who was, until her death, central to his intellectual and personal life. His writings, devoted to the humanising and widening of utilitarian teaching, include *System of Logic* (1843), *Principles of Political Economy* (1848) and his famous essay *On Liberty* (1859). In 1865 he was elected to Parliament and during his three years there defended, among many other causes, that of women's suffrage. His *Autobiography* was published in 1873, the year he died.

HARRIET TAYLOR MILL was born in 1808. In 1826 she married a wealthy London merchant, with whom she had two sons and a daughter. Her deep attachment to John Stuart Mill lasted from their first meeting until her death twenty-eight years later. They spent much time together – a situation accepted by her husband – and moved in two main social circles, The Philosophical Radicals and the Unitarian Radicals. In 1851, two years after her husband's death, they married. Harriet Taylor had an enormous effect on Mill's thinking and writings, particularly on the issues of social justice, personal liberty and the oppression of women. They wrote essays for each other on women's position in marriage and on divorce, in which Harriet Taylor argued against any laws on marriage, and for a woman taking responsibility for her own children. 'Enfranchisement of Women' was first published in 1851 in the *Westminster Review*. Both Harriet Taylor and Mill suffered from tuberculosis and she took numerous trips to Europe to try and improve her health. When Mill retired from the India Office (where he had worked all his life) in 1858, they set off for the south of France, but she fell ill on the journey and died at Avignon, where she is buried.

If you would like to know more about Virago books, write to us at 41 William IV Street, London WC2N 4DB for a full catalogue.

Please send a stamped addressed envelope

Book Tokens

Give them the pleasure of choosing

Book Tokens can be bought and exchanged at most bookshops.

ENFRANCHISEMENT
OF WOMEN

HARRIET TAYLOR MILL

&

THE
SUBJECTION OF WOMEN

JOHN STUART MILL

New Introduction by Kate Soper

Virago

Published by Virago Press Limited 1983
41 William IV Street, London WC2N 4DB

Enfranchisement of Women first published in 1851
The Subjection of Women first published in 1869
This edition of *The Subjection of Women* offset
from the Longmans, Green, Reader, and Dyer
edition of 1869
New Introduction copyright C Kate Soper 1983

Printed in Great Britain by litho at
The Anchor Press, Tiptree, Essex

British Library Cataloguing in Publication Data
Mill, John Stuart
The subjection of women: Enfranchisement of women.
1. Women's rights
I. Title   II. Mill, Harriet Taylor.
Enfranchisement of women
305.4'2   HQ1154

ISBN 0-86068-445-8

The cover shows portraits of John Stuart Mill
and Harriet Taylor Mill: in the background,
a detail from 'The House of Commons, 1858',
by Joseph Nash, reproduced by kind permission of
The Palace of Westminster Works of Art
Committee.

NEW INTRODUCTION

THREE quarters of a century separate Mary Wollstonecraft's *Vindication of the Rights of Women* (1792) from John Stuart Mill's *The Subjection of Women* (1869); yet in the annals of feminism it is as if they stand alongside, adjacent links in the chain of its literature. That the stature of Mill's essay, and its significance for feminists both in his own time and since, have been of this order, invites two rather differing lines of appraisal. In the first place it suggests that here we have a text of excelling quality and great intrinsic power. That Mill's work has seldom in this sense been rivalled is certainly true. But that it does stand in this isolation must be allowed to say something, too, of history's own marginalisation of the topic with which it deals. For what other subject of comparable importance has been found to have so few milestones charting its progress?

One very relevant instance (though one could cite many others) of the obscurity that has tended to shroud all but the most exceptional feminist writings is the neglect of the essay here attributed to Mill's wife, Harriet Taylor: the *Enfranchisement of Women*. Though an important piece of work, and written considerably earlier than *The Subjection*, it remains almost unread, and is only now published in a British edition together with the later work.[1]

Moreover in attaining the status of a 'classic', *The Subjection* has itself come to be invested with a timeless quality that can obscure the real history[2] of the attentions paid it – and which have been, in fact, very uneven and in some ways less of a response to the actual content of the essay than a reflection of the specific interests brought to its reading.

Though a work of maturity (it was in fact Mill's last published book[3]) by one of the most eminent and celebrated personalities of the day, it was greeted initially with intense hostility. The book was a source of embarrassment even to Mill's allies,[4] and the only one by him to lose him money. When it first began to win itself a wider and more enthusiastic readership it was in the early years of this century, and coincided with the main period of activity of the women's suffrage movement. New English and American editions of the essay were brought out during this period, that in England being published in 1912 in a selection of Mill's work introduced by the suffrage campaigner, Millicent Garrett Fawcett.[5] It has remained the standard source for the essay in this country ever since.

There is every reason, of course, why *The Subjection* should have become so closely associated with the literature of the franchise movement. Mill was known throughout his life as an uncompromising advocate of equal voting rights,[6] and in his period of office as a Member of Parliament (1865–68, between the writing and publication of *The Subjection*) had led the campaign in Parliament to amend the Second Reform Bill to include women within its terms. During the last years of his life he lent active support to his step-daughter, Helen Taylor (who played a leading role in the establishment of the National Society for Women's Suffrage), and together with her was closely involved in its organisation and politics.[7]

Nevertheless, the pleading of the suffrage cause occupies a very minor part of both essays, and is presented with the peremptoriness of those concerned to save their argument for the less blatantly obvious instances of injustice towards women. The central concern of the essays, in fact, is with nothing less fundamental than the subordination of women as such and its continual reproduction and reinforcement in the institution of marriage and the laws relating to it. And it is this which rendered them so out of joint with their times.

It is certainly true that the 'Woman Question' as interpreted by the Mills was a preoccupation of the progressive circles in which they moved, and was earnestly debated within them. It is true, too, that the followers of Saint-Simon and Robert Owen (both of them very influential on Mill's thinking) were actively canvassing in quite radical ways on behalf of women in the nineteenth century. Nonetheless, throughout that century and well into our own, it remained only a very small minority who were prepared to regard the issue of sexual equality as one touching on every aspect of women's existence.

It is in this sense, then, that one might want to claim that it is only now, when we are beginning to see a much more general acknowledgement both of the extent of the oppression of women and of the ways in which our society is constructed upon it, that these pioneering works are in a position to receive the serious and dispassionate reading they both deserve and require. Whatever other interests we may bring to them, it is not for us today a case of finding ourselves either shocked into dismissal of them by their radical daring, or else bound to endorse their every sentiment for fear of betraying the feminist cause. We can relate more directly to their actual content, and assess them on that grounds: we can treat them as representing specific forms of feminist *argument*, rather than feminism itself.

To judge by their own account, Harriet Taylor and John Stuart Mill enjoyed a well-nigh perfect communion together – in matters intellectual as in all else – for some twenty-one years (seven of them in marriage). It is therefore something of an irony that such discord has been sown between them posthumously by their commentators on the question of 'who wrote what?' and 'who, and for better or worse, influenced whom?' The essays printed here have by no means escaped this controversy. Not only is the nature of Harriet's contribution to *The Subjection* a matter of dispute, but her authorship of the *Enfranchisement* is itself contested.

On the issue of authorship, the essential facts are these. The *Enfranchisement of Women* was first published anonymously (as was the practise at the time) in the *Westminster Review* in 1851. Mill had referred to it in a letter to the editor of the *Review* as one *he* was preparing for publication.[8] Subsequently, in a letter to Harriet discussing his rejection of an offer to re-publish the article in 1854, he consoles her with the thought that it would appear in any subsequent collection of their articles, and would then be 'preceded by a preface which will show that much of all my later articles, and all the best of that one, were as they were, my Darling's'.[9] Yet the suggestion clearly given in these remarks that Mill regarded the work as his own is nonetheless confounded by the fact that in 1849 he had written to Harriet of the need for her to press ahead with her 'little book'. 'I do hope you are going on with it,' he writes, 'gone on with and finished and published it must be and next season too.'[10] Further endorsement of his wife's authorship is provided in his claim, on the re-printing of the essay after Harriet's death, that its authorship was 'known at the time, and publicly attributed to her'.[11]

Mill frankly acknowledges Harriet's contribution to his later work, *The Subjection*:

As ultimately published it was enriched with some important ideas of my daughter's, and passages of her writing. But in what was of my own composition, all that is most striking and profound belongs to my wife.[12]

That Mill in turn influenced the content of *Enfranchisement* and possibly had a hand in its writing, is indisputable; but since it is equally true that Harriet's ideas are at work in *The Subjection*, and that Mill published works under his sole authorship (for example, *The Principles of Political Economy*) to whose actual writing Harriet had contributed,[13] it seems only fair to credit her with authoring a work which was probably for the most part penned by her.[14]

It would be pointless here to add to the already extensive analysis of their relationship and overall influence upon one another.[15] Suffice it to say that to the extent it has bred controversy, this has primarily concerned the manner and extent of Harriet's influence over John, and with whether her genius was anything approaching that attributed to her by him. If one were to begin to take seriously Mill's claims that she was the 'greatest mind the century contained'[16] and he the mere 'mediator' of ideas originating in her,[17] then perhaps our concern should be rather more for the effects that the encounter with Mill may have had on her development! But if few have worried unduly about what Harriet might have been had she not devoted her life to his genius, much ink has been spilled over what Mill might have been without her.

On the whole, both in Mill's own day and since, the judgement has not been very friendly towards Harriet. Several of Mill's contemporaries are on record as finding rather little in her to recommend, and the majority of Mill's commentators since have preferred to find any other explanation for the extravagance of Mill's praise of her rather than believe it. In doing so, they express the doubts vented by Mill's friend and biographer, Alexander

Bain, who pleaded (in vain) with Mill to tone down the eulogy of her in his *Autobiography* lest it discredit him, and on the appearance of that work in 1873 suggested that such a combination of talents as Mill found in Harriet 'has never been realised in the history of the human race.'[18] Bain's ultimate assessment of Harriet, on the other hand, is by no means hostile, and on the whole the more sensitive commentary since on their relationship has also been the more charitable towards her. In her important interpretative work on Mill's liberalism, Gertrude Himmelfarb has emphasised Harriet's role in its development and the impact of her ideas on the making of the essay *On Liberty*.[19]

A valuable contribution to the discussion of Harriet's personality has been made by Alice Rossi, who draws our attention to the personal and political considerations affecting the judgements upon it. She argues persuasively, for example, that the negative assessments of Harriet tend to come primarily from the Philosophic Radicals and reflect their fears for Mill's absorption in the circle of Unitarian Radicals to which Harriet belonged.[20] Less conventional and more utopian than the Philosophic Radicals in their thinking about social change (particularly on the issue of women and the family), the Unitarians were at odds in many ways with the views and methods of the Utilitarianism; we can well believe that Mill's friends (who remained largely unaware of the challenge Mill's own mental crisis had already delivered to his Utilitarianism[21] by the time he met Harriet), were wary of the impact upon him of Harriet's more passionate, more radical and in certain respects more elitist[22] approach to society and its wrongs.

There is some reason to associate these differences in political orientation with the differences in argument that are to be found in the essays on sexual equality.

It is relevant in this connection to point out the relative absence from the *Enfranchisement* of the difficulties affecting the argument of *The Subjection* as a result of the latter's attempt to reconcile Utilitarian arguments for equality with its attack upon the injustice of the oppression of women. On the one hand, *The Subjection* argues (and very cogently) that there can never be any appeal to custom or experience to justify the subordination of women, and that their right to equality is established independently of any consideration of their 'nature' or current desires; on the other hand, the essay also invites us to accept the evidence of 'experience' that women's 'nature' is indeed different from men's – and that it is, is one of the reasons why they and society will gain in happiness from their emancipation. Anyone who wants to argue, as Mill does, both that women's character is an 'eminently artificial thing', a product of culture to which no appeal can be made in judging their claim to equal treatment, while at the same time invoking the evidence of that very 'nature' in support of the case for liberation, is clearly open to attack on the grounds of inconsistency.[23]

It is true that the *Enfranchisement*, while it puts most weight on the injustice of treating any individual as inferior simply on the basis of the accident of gender, is also concerned to emphasise the happiness that will ensue from sexual equality. But the argument for this is more exclusively based than it is in *The Subjection* on a theoretical projection of the altered desires that would follow upon a change in women's circumstances, and is not made to depend in any way on the truth of claims regarding the character or inclinations of women as such.

Insofar, however, as both the *Enfranchisement* and *The Subjection* tend to suggest that the oppression of women is the more unjust in the 'modern world' for being more discordant with its general practice, both might be accused of compromising on the argument for its *absolute* injustice. For it is, in fact, a pervasive theme of both essays that it is only recently that conditions have become propitious for any practical implementation of women's right to equality.

In *The Subjection*, for example, much of the early argument is devoted to exposing the wholly anachronistic nature of the existing power relations between men and women, where, it is suggested, absolutism and commitment to the principle that 'might is right' stand out in stark contrast to the dissolution of their hold upon other areas of life, thus making of the law of servitude in marriage,

a monstrous contradiction to all the principles of the modern world, and to all the experience through which those principles have been slowly and painfully worked out. (p. 147)

The *Enfranchisement*, somewhat more optimistically, chooses to stress not so much the persistence of an anomalous form of despotism, but the improved 'moral sentiments' and changes in taste and habit that render the times opportune for dispensing with it. It claims that

an increased sense of the consideration due by every man to those who have no one but himself to look to, has tended to make the home more and more the centre of interest, and domestic circumstances and society a larger and larger part of life, and of its pursuits and pleasures. (p. 27)

This, combined with declining appetite on the part of men for the 'violent bodily exercises, noisy merriment and intemperance' that were their former gratifications, has brought about a situation in which 'for the first time in the world, men and women are really companions' (p. 27). While this growth in association has so far proceeded only at the cost of a certain domestification of the male (whose 'enfeeblement' and loss of public-spiritedness as a result of closer contact with their wives is a topic of concern of both essays[24]), the suggestion is that it has nonetheless laid the essential grounds for the transformation of the marriage union into a relationship of equals.

Since one of the main effects for middle-class women of the industrial revolution was to confine them to the distinctive role of 'adorning' the household that it fell to the separate task of men to support, while on men and women of the working-class it imposed such intensive exploitation that there was little time or energy left for any genuine 'companionship', we may find this argument somewhat abstract. To understand the weight placed on it by the Mills, we must understand the structural importance to their whole argument for the emancipation of women of their faith in the progressive nature of liberal society. For the fundamental grounds upon which it is claimed that the modern age is in a position to release society from its relics of barbarism, is the freedom and equality permitted to the individual by the replacement of a pre-ordained, aristocratic ordering of society by a system of market relations based on competition. The peculiar character of the modern world, says Mill, is that in it

human beings are no longer born to their place in life and chained down by an inexorable bond to the place they are born to, but are free to employ their faculties, and such favourable chances as offer, to achieve the lot which may appear to them most desirable. (pp. 29–30)

There is much in Harriet's essay that agrees with *The Subjection* in its approval of a world where the individual is freed from chivalry, charity and any other form of patronage, and accorded the dignity of one who 'is able to take care of himself' (p. 159). Yet the *Enfranchisement* is both more wary of this new principle of competition and less abstract in discussing it. Thus, on the one hand, it sees fit to deal with some of the more practical and very topical objections to allowing women to compete (that this will flood the labour market, thus depressing wages; that it will conflict with maternity) while at the same time arguing

with respect to the future, we neither believe that improvident multiplication, and the consequent excessive difficulties of gaining a subsistence, will always continue, nor that the division of mankind into capitalists and hired labourers, and the regulation of the reward of labourers mainly by demand and supply, will be for ever, or even much longer the rule of the world. (p. 21)

We can associate with this critique of the liberal case for female equality a substantial difference between the essays over the issue of female employment. For while the *Enfranchisement* draws the logical conclusion from the endorsement of the principle of competition that women, to be truly free of the tyranny of protectionism, must be allowed to support themselves materially and to contribute on equal terms to the family income, *The Subjection* is less than consistent on this point. Acknowledging that it is essential to the 'dignity' of women that they be enabled to work and earn their living if need be (p. 89), Mill nonetheless argues that it is undesirable that they should do so in fact:

the common arrangement, by which the man earns the income and the wife superintends the domestic expenditure . . . seems the most suitable division of labour between the two persons. (pp. 87–88)

It is true that Harriet's more forthright approach to this issue goes along with a certain insensitivity to the immensity of the obstacles to combining maternity with the pursuit of a career. We may also feel that she is too ready to privilege intellectual self-fulfilment over every other form of gratification. Mill, on the other hand, more sensitive to the tensions here but more of an idealist about the capacity of 'compatible minds' to overcome them, can be equally criticised for concentrating overmuch on the removal of the legal forms of oppression and too little on the material factors underlying the inequality of women before the law. One hesitates, however, to make too much of this criticism when at the time of his writing women were legally little better off than bond-slaves.

Kate Millett has rightly drawn attention to the onslaught that *The Subjection* represented not only from the legal standpoint, but upon the Victorian ideology of the home as haven from the hurly-burly of the market place together with all its nauseous idolatry-cum-infantilisation of the 'Woman' who reigned 'sovereign' within its bounds.[25] There is no doubt that Mill's 'strenuous realism' cuts like a knife through Ruskin's unctuous paeon to Victorian womanliness in 'Of Queen's Gardens' and all similar pieties.[26] But in pointing to the contrast here, we should not overlook the fact that while Mill is completely committed *intellectually* to the removal of all forms of discrimination be-tween the sexes, he is resistant to any break-up of traditional family life, and on the whole approving of its existing division of labour.

This is not the only point in his argument where Mill's subjective preferences and attitudes are allowed to get the better of his reasoning. Had he, for example, been less inclined to place that trust in his own instincts that he finds so deplorable in his opponents, then perhaps he would have thought more deeply about the ease with which he depicts men of the lower classes as more naturally brutal towards their women than their more educated middle-class 'superiors'. (p. 84)

Perhaps, too, he would have been less inclined to fly in the face of all his own advice that it would be 'presumption in anyone to pretend to decide what women are or are not, can or cannot be by any natural constitution' (p. 104), by inviting us to accept a good part of the received wisdom regarding the character of women and their 'natural' proclivities. Mill's tendency, in fact, is not so much to reject the traditional depiction of women, as to challenge the correctness of the assumptions that are made on its basis regard-ing the capacities of women to engage in public life. We have already noted how uneasily such arguments combine with the rationale of his attack on bourgeois society for its naturalisation of custom.

In contrast to this defence of women's particular talents is the greater impatience of the *Enfranchisement* with any rhetoric that would have us see women apart as a 'sort of sentimental priest-hood'. (p. 42) Briskly denouncing any 'verbiage' serving to mar the 'simplicity and rationality' of the demand for equal treatment, it argues:

> The strength of the cause lies in the support of those who are influenced by reason and principle; and to attempt to recommend it by sentimentalities, absurd in reason, and inconsistent with the principle on which the movement is founded, is to place a good cause on a level with a bad one. (p. 42)

If Mill agreed with all the arguments of the *Enfranchisement* at the time of its writing, then there is no doubt that he had modified his views in some respects by the time he came to write *The Subjection*. For the latter differs from the *Enfranchisement* not only in its attitude to domestic arrangements, but in the absence from it of the latter's more 'socialist' vein of comment on the principle of competition, and on many more nuanced points as well. While Mill himself (especially while Harriet was alive) on many occasions professed his support for 'Socialism'[27], one nevertheless comes away from *The Subjection* with the feeling that Harriet might have found it guilty of a measure of that 'moderate reformism' with which the *Enfranchisement* acknowledges its own collision.

In this context, however, it is worth pointing out that the 'Socialism' that Harriet and John professed owed little or nothing to the Marxist critique of capitalist society. One relevant example (though it by no means exhausts the differences here) is the influence of Malthus on their support for policies of birth control. The Philosophic Radicals were enthusiasts of Malthusianism, interpreting it in the progressive sense that it 'indicated the indefinite improvability of human affairs by securing full employment at high wages to the whole labouring population through a voluntary restriction of the increase of their numbers'.[28] This was quite against the grain of Marx and Engels and their followers, who associated Malthusian doctrine with the errors of bourgeois political economy. According to them, in 'proving' that the workers' increasing immiseration followed necessarily upon an increase in their numbers, Malthus was merely offering an apologetic that concealed its real cause in specifically capitalist relations of production and their exploitation of the mass of the population. (Insofar as the Marxist opposition to Malthus became an opposition to contraception, it bred a longstanding controversy between socialists and birth controllers.[29])

That *The Subjection* was greeted with general hostility and even contempt at the time of its publication is hardly remarkable. Nor were the objectors exclusively male – some of the more eloquent dismissals of Millian argument were written by Mrs Oliphant and Anne Mozley, who found Mill guilty of an insufferable combination of arrogance (in presuming to know what women really are and want) and fanciful utopianism (in aspiring to alter an arrangement ordained by nature). Mrs Oliphant, both in a review of *The Subjection* and in an earlier article deriding Mill's championship of female householders at the time of the Second Reform Bill,[30] spares no irony in her attack on the 'abstraction' of the 'philosopher's' logic. In doing so, she reflects what was a very widespread characterisation of Mill, the 'reasoning machine', whose words one might have to respect in matters speculative, but who had very little sense of the lovable, if illogical, sentiments that were the cement of the real world of flesh and blood individuals.

The portrayal of Mill as a mere engine of logic was certainly a caricature and hardly borne out by the reactions of some of his feminist readers. There is no doubt, however, that in explaining the resistance to the programme advocated by the Mills, we need to point not only to its progressive radicalism but also to the *type* of argument upon which it is based. It was a common charge against Utilitarianism that it made its appeal too exclusively to reason and showed too little appreciation of 'feeling'. The impatience with any explanation invoking sentiment or received opinion, while very healthy in some respects, went together nonetheless with an overly positivistic approach to psychology and a tendency to deny the full range of emotions at play in determining the relations between the sexes.

Though Mill, as I have indicated, was not entirely free of the Victorian idealisation of women, he remained unaware both of the full seductiveness of its image for his contemporaries and of its function in bourgeois society. Reason in the end persuades him that education and the cultivation of right thinking will triumph over all opposition between what it is reasonable to do and what is actually done.

This privileging of reason no doubt bears in complex ways on Harriet and John's attitude to physical sex and sensual passion – which they portray as, if not exactly unworthy of the true union, by no means essential to it. While their anti-eroticism was no exception to the general rule of feminist thinking of their day, one can imagine that a certain amount of potential support for their arguments may have been alienated by the condescension of their attitude to physical love.

What is likely to jar most on today's readers, however, is the central argument of the essays that sees the issue of female rights primarily in terms of the opportunity equality will allow for individually talented women to emerge to prominence and realise fulfilment. This is a theme in conflict with that strand of the contemporary women's movement, which stresses not the individual's right to compete, but the iniquity of the competition itself, and which appeals to a collective identity for women in their common struggle against patriarchy. (Gertrude Himmelfarb, in this connection, has suggested that Mill's essay is often mistakenly enlisted by feminists in support of a cause he never espoused.)

On the other hand, there could hardly be a more eloquent reinforcement of the anti-separatist position than in Mill's argument that it is not men who are the prime oppressors of women, but the tradition and custom of society. It is with this conviction – that the subjection of women is a common problem of humanity – that we must associate the negative assessments to be found in both essays of the effects that enslaved women have on their masters, the insistence with which they maintain that the liberation of men can only come about with sexual equality, and the appeal they make to men to join forces in attaining it. (p. 145)

The pertinence of this line of argument to the present day concerns of the women's movement scarcely needs stressing. But it by no means exhausts the contemporary relevance of the essays. Together they touch on those central issues that structure the debate on women and render all sloganising appeals to their 'rights' or 'equality' more problematic than might at first appear. The question of the differences between the sexes, and the respective roles of nature and culture in their formation; the question of distinctive feminine 'values' and their actual existence or symbolic role; the question of the extent of women's 'rights' and the politics of the appeal to them: all these are issues very much alive today to whose discussion these essays have a definite contribution to make. Equally alive is the vexed issue they raise of the compatibility of the more reformist struggles with the fight for the radical social changes that many believe to be the condition of genuine female emancipation.

However great the disagreement with these essays in their detail or in their substance, no one who reads them, one suspects, will be anything but grateful for their eloquent presentation of the liberal case on women. While students of political and social theory and of nineteenth century history and culture will also, one hopes, welcome the easy access this volume provides to the thought on a vital and ramified topic of two of the more outstanding figures of Victorian society.

Kate Soper, Rodmell, 1983

I am grateful to Rosalind Delmar, Cora Kaplan, Trevor Pateman, Martin H. Ryle and Barbara Taylor for assistance with this introduction.

NOTES

1 The *Enfranchisement* and *The Subjection of Women* were first published together (along with two *Early Essays on Marriage and Divorce*) in an American edition introduced by Alice S. Rossi, The University of Chicago Press, Chicago, 1970.

2 Letter to Harriet Taylor (after Oct. 29 1850), in *The Later Letters of John Stuart Mill*, eds. Francis E. Mineka and Dwight N. Lindley, *Collected Works of John Stuart Mill* (*CW*), University of Toronto Press, Routledge and Kegan Paul, 1972 – , Vol. XIV, p. 49. The relegation of *The Subjection* to the status of a minor *opus* in the *oeuvre* is reflected both in its publishing record and in the dearth of serious attention paid its argument. A recent study of Mill's social thought (F. L. von Holthoon, *The Road to Utopia*, Assen, Von Gorcum and Comp. N.V., 1971) does not even refer to it. But for two very substantial analyses of its argument, see Julia Annas, 'Mill and the Subjection of Women', *Philosophy* 52, 1977 and Susan Moller Okin, *Women in Western Political Thought*, Virago, London, 1980, Chap. 9 (particularly valuable in revealing the range of influences that went into the making of Mill's position on women).

3 Written in 1861, it was withheld from publication until 1869. Mill died in 1873.

4 In his *Life of John Stuart Mill* (Secker and Warburg, London 1964) M. St John Packe tells us there was more antagonism to *The Subjection* than to any other of Mill's works; see also the biography of

Mill by his friend Alexander Bain: *John Stuart Mill*, London, 1882, p. 108.

5   *On Liberty, The Subjection of Women*, etc., introd. by Millicent Garrett Fawcett, The World's Classics, Oxford University Press, London, 1912.

6   He makes it clear in his *Autobiography* (ed. Jack Stillinger, Oxford University Press, London, 1969, p. 63 and p. 147) that Harriet had no influence upon him in this respect, and that his support for female franchise dated from his earliest days; in arguing for the vote for women, Mill departed from the view of his father, James Mill, whose opposition to women's suffrage had proved the occasion in 1825 for William Thompson's impassioned *Appeal to One Half of the Human Race, Men*, Virago, London, 1983. John Stuart Mill, of course, no more supported universal franchise for women than he did for men.

7   See *Autobiography ed. cit.*, pp. 165–185 on Mill's career in Parliament and his association with Helen Taylor. For some fascinating insights on Helen Taylor's role and influence after her mother's death, see Mineka and Lindley introd. to the *Later Letters, op. cit.*, pp. xxxiv–xxxvii.

8   *Later Letters, op. cit.*, p. 56.

9   *Ibid.*, p. 190.

10 *Ibid.*, p. 13.

11 *Dissertations and Discussions*, Parker and Son, London, 1859, Vol. II, p. 411.

12 *Autobiography, ed. cit.*, p. 158.

13 Harriet's part in the *Political Economy* is generally acknowledged. The letters between her and John relating to its content are some of the more interesting, throwing light as they do on the conduct of their disputes with each other (see letters 5, 6, 8, 9, 10 in *Later Letters*).

14 It is not only the content of the essay that is evidence of this but its similarity in style to Harriet Taylor's earlier 'private' essay on marriage and divorce (printed in Rossi, *ed. cit.*).

15 In addition to A. Bain, *op. cit.*, St John Packe, *op. cit.*, A. Rossi's introd., *op. cit.*, see G. Himmelfarb, *On Liberty and Liberalism*, Alfred A. Knopf, New York, 1974, Jack Stillinger, introd. to *The Early Draft of John Stuart Mill's "Autobiography"*, University of Illinois Press, Urbana, 1961; F. A. Hayek, *John Stuart Mill and Harriet Taylor*, Routledge and Kegan Paul, London, 1951; Francis E. Mineka, ed. *The Early Letters of John Stuart Mill, CW*, Vol. XII; H. O. Pappe, *John Stuart Mill and the Harriet Taylor Myth*, Melbourne, 1960.

16 *Later Letters*, vol. XV, p. 601.

17 *Autobiography, ed. cit.*, p. 112.

18 Letter from A. Bain to Helen Taylor, Sept. 6 1873 in J. Stillinger ed. *The Early Draft*, *cit.*, p. 73.

19 G. Himmelfarb, *op. cit.*, especially Part II.

20 A. Rossi *ed. cit.*, pp. 31–38; see also F. Mineka, *The Dissidence of Dissent*, University of North Carolina Press, Chapel Hill, 1944, and M. Hamburger's informative work: *Intellectuals in Politics: John Stuart Mill and the Philosophic Radicals*, Yale University Press, Newhaven and London, 1965. Though sharing much in common, the Unitarians were more anarchist in their thinking than were the Utilitarians and less prepared than they to engage in Parliamentary politics. (Mary Wollstonecraft, associate of William Godwin, had been a Unitarian.) The Taylor household was a main meeting place in the 1830s for the Unitarian Radicals, who included among their number at the time, the Unitarian minister, William Fox, Eliza and Sarah Flower, William Adams and Harriet Martineau. Their organ was the *Monthly Repository*, edited by Fox. Drawing their inspiration from the Utilitarianism of James Mill and Jeremy Bentham, the Philosophic Radicals had constituted themselves with the aim of cementing an alliance between the middle and working classes against the aristocracy. Commenting on the failure of their political efforts during the 1830s to supplant the Whigs as a 'People's' Party of opposition to the Tories, Hamburger writes: 'They had assumed the People existed, yet finally Chartism and middle-class apathy and fear of the working classes showed them that the People was not a unitary body' (p. 263). Prominent in their circle were John Roebuck, George and Harriet Grote, Charles and Sarah Austin, Francis Place, Sydney Smith, Joseph Hume, Charles Buller and a number of other notable figures in British politics of the time. Their journal was the *Westminster Review*.

21 On this, see his *Autobiography*, p. 80f where he charts the effects of his disillusionment in 1826 with Benthamite Utilitarianism and the solace he drew from the Romantic poets. That Mill's 'crisis' must be directly linked to his treatment by his father and his unhappy relations with both parents, seems indisputable. (Its psychoanalytic implications were first explored by A. W. Levi, "The Mental Crisis of John Stuart Mill", *Psychoanalytic Review*, 32, pp. 86–101). A similar link can no doubt be claimed to hold in regard to Mill's strong identification with the cause of women.

22 As evidenced, for example, in her contempt for conformity, privileging of the intellect and commitment to the development of individuality as the supreme value. In her early essay on marriage, she suggests to Mill that there is 'but one class' to whom the highest virtues can be taught: 'the poetic nature struggling with superstition: you are fitted to be the saviour of such.'

23   And is so attacked, quite forcibly, by Julia Annas, *art. cit.*

24   Trevor Pateman has suggested to me that this surely derives from
     Mill's pro-Greek orientation; in Greek political thought men are
     men *because* they are *citizens*, and virtue is essentially *civic* virtue. On
     Mill's debt to Plato and Aristotle, see Pateman's article in *Radical
     Philosophy*, no. 32.

25   See Kate Millett, *Sexual Politics*, Virago Press, London, 1977, p. 89f.

26   'Of Queen's Gardens' is included in *Sesame and Lilies*, Ruskin's
     most popular work at the time. The *locus classicus* for such sen-
     timentalisation of 'Woman' is Coventry Patmore's poem of 1855,
     'The Angel in the House'; see also Tennyson's *Idylls of the King*, and
     (in rather more banal vein) Samuel Smiles on 'Companionship in
     Marriage' in his work *Character*, 1872.

27   We find him, for example, writing to Harriet in 1849: 'Progress of
     the right kind seems to me to be quite safe now that Socialism has
     become inextinguishable' (*Later Letters*, *op. cit.*, p. 21); discussing
     Harriet's influence on his thought in his *Autobiography*, he mentions
     a shift to a 'qualified Socialism' as one of the more substantial
     changes she introduced (p. 115 and cf. p. 138).

28   *Autobiography*, p. 64; cf. the pro-Malthusian argument of the chapter
     (attributed to Harriet) on the future of the labouring classes in the
     Principles of Political Economy, *CW*, vol. III, pp. 765–66. In her
     approving remarks on the foresight shown by the Mills on the issue
     of birth control, Rossi, to my mind, shows too little awareness of the
     controversial aspects of the case they make for it (*ed. cit.*, pp. 53–56).

29   For a fuller discussion on the arguments around the issue of birth
     control in the nineteenth century, see J. A. and O. Banks, *Feminism
     and Family Planning in Victorian England*, Liverpool University Press,
     1964; A. McClaren, *Birth Control in Nineteenth Century England*,
     Croom Helm, London, 1978; J. Weeks, *Sex, Politics and Society: the
     Regulation of Sexuality since 1800*, Longmans, London, 1981.

30   Contrary to Mill's fond supposition, claims Oliphant, this staid and
     middle-aged group of women, who alone would benefit from his
     amendment, have no desire 'to descend to the poll with the green-
     grocer', nor feel themselves less than perfect for being something
     other than a repetition of the male. Her article, 'The Great Unrep-
     resented' appeared in Blackwoods Magazine in 1866 and was
     followed by a review of *The Subjection* printed in the *Edinburgh Review*
     in 1869. Anne Mozley's review appeared the same year in *Blackwoods
     Magazine*.
        We might note that in 1889 'An Appeal against Female Suffrage'
     received the signatures of about 100 women, many of them promin-
     ent public figures.

ENFRANCHISEMENT
OF WOMEN

ENFRANCHISEMENT
OF WOMEN

Introduction by John Stuart Mill to the reprinting of *Enfranchisement of Women* (1851) in his collection *Dissertations and Discussions* (1859).

All the more recent of these papers were joint productions of myself and of one whose loss, even in a merely intellectual point of view, can never be repaired or alleviated. But the following Essay is hers in a peculiar sense, my share in it being little more than that of an editor and amanuensis. Its authorship having been known at the time, and publicly attributed to her, it is proper to state, that she never regarded it as a complete discussion of the subject which it treats of: and, highly as I estimate it, I would rather it remained unacknowledged, than that it should be read with the idea that even the faintest image can be found in it of a mind and heart which in their union of the rarest, and what are deemed the most conflicting excellences, were unparalleled in any human being that I have known or read of. While she was the light, life, and grace of every society in which she took part, the foundation of her character was a deep seriousness, resulting from the combination of the strongest and most sensitive feelings with the highest principles. All that excites admiration when found separately in others, seemed brought together in her: a conscience at once healthy and tender; a generosity, bounded only by a sense of justice which often forgot its own claims, but never those of others; a heart so large and loving, that whoever was capable

of making the smallest return of sympathy, always
received tenfold; and in the intellectual department,
a vigour and truth of imagination, a delicacy of
perception, an accuracy and nicety of observation,
only equalled by her profundity of speculative
thought, and by a practical judgment and discernment
next to infallible. So elevated was the general level of
her faculties, that the highest poetry, philosophy,
oratory, or art, seemed trivial by the side of her, and
equal only to expressing some small part of her mind.
And there is no one of those modes of manifestation in
which she could not easily have taken the highest rank,
had not her inclination led her for the most part to
content herself with being the inspirer, prompter, and
unavowed coadjutor of others.

The present paper was written to promote a cause
which she had deeply at heart, and though appealing
only to the severest reason, was meant for the general
reader. The question, in her opinion, was in a stage in
which no treatment but the most calmly argumentative could be useful, while many of the strongest
arguments were necessarily omitted, as being un-
suited for popular effect. Had she lived to write out
all her thoughts on this great question, she would have
produced something as far transcending in profundity
the present Essay, as, had she not placed a rigid
restraint on her feelings, she would have excelled it in
fervid eloquence. Yet nothing which even she could
have written on any single subject, would have given
an adequate idea of the depth and compass of her
mind. As during life she continually detected, before
any one else had seemed to perceive them, those
changes of times and circumstances which ten or
twelve years later became subjects of general remark,
so I venture to prophecy that if mankind continue to
improve, their spiritual history for ages to come will
be the progressive working out of her thoughts, and
realization of her conceptions.

*   *   *

Most of our readers will probably learn from these pages for the first time, that there has arisen in the United States, and in the most civilized and enlightened portion of them, an organized agitation on a new question—new, not to thinkers, nor to any one by whom the principles of free and popular government are felt as well as acknowledged, but new, and even unheard-of, as a subject for public meetings and practical political action. This question is, the enfranchisement of women; their admission, in law and in fact, to equality in all rights, political, civil, and social, with the male citizens of the community.

It will add to the surprise with which many will receive this intelligence, that the agitation which has commenced is not a pleading by male writers and orators for women, those who are professedly to be benefited remaining either indifferent or ostensibly hostile. It is a political movement, practical in its objects, carried on in a form which denotes an intention to persevere. And it is a movement not merely *for* women, but *by* them. Its first public manifestation appears to have been a Convention of Women, held in the State of Ohio, in the spring of 1850. Of this meeting we have seen no report. On the 23rd and 24th of October last, a succession of public meetings was held at Worcester in Massachusetts under the name of a "Women's Rights Convention," of which the president was a woman, and nearly all the chief speakers women: numerously reinforced, however, by men, among

whom were some of the most distinguished
leaders in the kindred cause of negro emancipation. A general and four special committees
were nominated, for the purpose of carrying on
the undertaking until the next annual meeting.

According to the report in the *New York
Tribune*, above a thousand persons were present
throughout, and "if a larger place could have
been had, many thousands more would have
attended." The place was described as "crowded
from the beginning with attentive and interested
listeners." In regard to the quality of the
speaking, the proceedings bear an advantageous
comparison with those of any popular movement
with which we are acquainted, either in this
country or in America. Very rarely in the
oratory of public meetings is the part of verbiage
and declamation so small, that of calm good
sense and reason so considerable. The result of
the Convention was in every respect encouraging to those by whom it was summoned: and
it is probably destined to inaugurate one of the
most important of the movements towards
political and social reform, which are the best
characteristics of the present age.

That the promoters of this new agitation take
their stand on principles, and do not fear to
declare these in their widest extent, without
time-serving or compromise, will be seen from
the resolutions adopted by the Convention, part
of which we transcribe.

Resolved—That every human being, of full age, and
resident for a proper length of time on the soil of the

nation, who is required to obey the law, is entitled to a voice in its enactment; that every such person, whose property or labour is taxed for the support of the government, is entitled to a direct share in such government; therefore,

Resolved—That women are entitled to the right of suffrage, and to be considered eligible to office, . . . and that every party which claims to represent the humanity, the civilization, and the progress of the age, is bound to inscribe on its banners equality before the law, without distinction of sex or colour.

Resolved—That civil and political rights acknowledge no sex, and therefore the word "male" should be struck from every State Constitution.

Resolved—That, since the prospect of honourable and useful employment in after-life is the best stimulus to the use of educational advantages, and since the best education is that we give ourselves, in the struggles, employments, and discipline of life; therefore it is impossible that women should make full use of the instruction already accorded to them, or that their career should do justice to their faculties, until the avenues to the various civil and professional employments are thrown open to them.

Resolved—That every effort to educate women, without according to them their rights, and arousing their conscience by the weight of their responsibilities, is futile, and a waste of labour.

Resolved—That the laws of property, as affecting married persons, demand a thorough revisal, so that all rights be equal between them; that the wife have, during life, an equal control over the property gained by their mutual toil and sacrifices, and be heir to her husband precisely to that extent that he is heir to her, and entitled at her death to dispose by will of the same share of the joint property as he is.

The following is a brief summary of the principal demands.

1. *Education* in primary and high schools, universities, medical, legal, and theological institutions.
2. *Partnership* in the labours and gains, risks and remunerations, of productive industry.
3. *A coequal share* in the formation and administration of laws—municipal, state, and national—through legislative assemblies, courts, and executive offices.

It would be difficult to put so much true, just, and reasonable meaning into a style so little calculated to recommend it as that of some of the resolutions. But whatever objection may be made to some of the expressions, none, in our opinion, can be made to the demands themselves. As a question of justice, the case seems to us too clear for dispute. As one of expediency, the more thoroughly it is examined the stronger it will appear.

That women have as good a claim as men have, in point of personal right, to the suffrage, or to a place in the jury-box, it would be difficult for any one to deny. It cannot certainly be denied by the United States of America, as a people or as a community. Their democratic institutions rest avowedly on the inherent right of every one to a voice in the government. Their Declaration of Independence, framed by the men who are still their great constitutional authorities—that document which has been from the first, and is now, the acknowledged basis of their polity, commences with this express statement:

We hold these truths to be self-evident: that all men are created equal; that they are endowed by their

Creator with certain inalienable rights; that among
these are life, liberty, and the pursuit of happiness;
that to secure these rights, governments are instituted
among men, deriving their just powers from the
consent of the governed.

We do not imagine that any American demo-
crat will evade the force of these expressions by
the dishonest or ignorant subterfuge, that
"men," in this memorable document, does not
stand for human beings, but for one sex only;
that "life, liberty, and the pursuit of happiness"
are "inalienable rights" of only one moiety of
the human species; and that "the governed,"
whose consent is affirmed to be the only source
of just power, are meant for that half of mankind
only, who, in relation to the other, have hitherto
assumed the character of governors. The contradiction between principle and practice cannot be
explained away. A like dereliction of the fundamental maxims of their political creed has been
committed by the Americans in the flagrant
instance of the negroes; of this they are learning
to recognise the turpitude. After a struggle
which, by many of its incidents, deserves the
name of heroic, the abolitionists are now so
strong in numbers and in influence that they
hold the balance of parties in the United States.
It was fitting that the men whose names will
remain associated with the extirpation, from the
democratic soil of America, of the aristocracy of
colour, should be among the originators, for
America and for the rest of the world, of the first
collective protest against the aristocracy of sex;

a distinction as accidental as that of colour, and fully as irrelevant to all questions of government.

Not only to the democracy of America, the claim of women to civil and political equality makes an irresistible appeal, but also to those Radicals and Chartists in the British islands, and democrats on the Continent, who claim what is called universal suffrage as an inherent right, unjustly and oppressively withheld from them. For with what truth or rationality could the suffrage be termed universal, while half the human species remained excluded from it? To declare that a voice in the government is the right of all, and demand it only for a part—the part, namely, to which the claimant himself belongs—is to renounce even the appearance of principle. The Chartist who denies the suffrage to women, is a Chartist only because he is not a lord: he is one of those levellers who would level only down to themselves.

Even those who do not look upon a voice in the government as a matter of personal right, nor profess principles which require that it should be extended to all, have usually traditional maxims of political justice with which it is impossible to reconcile the exclusion of all women from the common rights of citizenship. It is an axiom of English freedom that taxation and representation should be co-extensive. Even under the laws which give the wife's property to the husband, there are many unmarried women who pay taxes. It is one of the fundamental doctrines of the British Constitution, that all

persons should be tried by their peers: yet
women, whenever tried, are tried by male judges
and a male jury. To foreigners the law accords
the privilege of claiming that half the jury should
be composed of themselves; not so to women.
Apart from maxims of detail, which represent
local and national rather than universal ideas;
it is an acknowledged dictate of justice to make
no degrading distinctions without necessity. In
all things the presumption ought to be on the
side of equality. A reason must be given why
anything should be permitted to one person and
interdicted to another. But when that which is
interdicted includes nearly everything which
those to whom it is permitted most prize, and
to be deprived of which they feel to be most
insulting; when not only political liberty but
personal freedom of action is the prerogative of
a caste; when even in the exercise of industry,
almost all employments which task the higher
faculties in an important field, which lead to
distinction, riches, or even pecuniary independence, are fenced round as the exclusive
domain of the predominant section, scarcely any
doors being left open to the dependent class,
except such as all who can enter elsewhere dis-
dainfully pass by; the miserable expediencies
which are advanced as excuses for so grossly
partial a dispensation, would not be sufficient,
even if they were real, to render it other than a
flagrant injustice. While, far from being expedient, we are firmly convinced that the division
of mankind into two castes, one born to rule

over the other, is in this case, as in all cases, an unqualified mischief; a source of perversion and demoralization, both to the favoured class and to those at whose expense they are favoured; producing none of the good which it is the custom to ascribe to it, and forming a bar, almost insuperable while it lasts, to any really vital improvement, either in the character or in the social condition of the human race.

These propositions it is now our purpose to maintain. But before entering on them, we would endeavour to dispel the preliminary objections which, in the minds of persons to whom the subject is new, are apt to prevent a real and conscientious examination of it. The chief of these obstacles is that most formidable one, custom. Women never have had equal rights with men. The claim in their behalf, of the common rights of mankind, is looked upon as barred by universal practice. This strongest of prejudices, the prejudice against what is new and unknown, has, indeed, in an age of changes like the present, lost much of its force; if it had not, there would be little hope of prevailing against it. Over three-fourths of the habitable world, even at this day, the answer, "it has always been so," closes all discussion. But it is the boast of modern Europeans, and of their American kindred, that they know and do many things which their forefathers neither knew nor did; and it is perhaps the most unquestionable point of superiority in the present above former ages, that habit is not now the tyrant it formerly was over opinions and

modes of action, and that the worship of custom
is a declining idolatry. An uncustomary thought,
on a subject which touches the greater interests
of life, still startles when first presented; but if
it can be kept before the mind until the impression of strangeness wears off, it obtains a
hearing, and as rational a consideration as the
intellect of the hearer is accustomed to bestow on
any other subject.

In the present case, the prejudice of custom is
doubtless on the unjust side. Great thinkers,
indeed, at different times, from Plato to Con-
dorcet, besides some of the most eminent names
of the present age, have made emphatic protests
in favour of the equality of women. And there
have been voluntary societies, religious or
secular, of which the Society of Friends is the
most known, by whom that principle was
recognised. But there has been no political
community or nation in which, by law and usage,
women have not been in a state of political and
civil inferiority. In the ancient world the same
fact was alleged, with equal truth, in behalf of
slavery. It might have been alleged in favour of
the mitigated form of slavery, serfdom, all
through the middle ages. It was urged against
freedom of industry, freedom of conscience, freedom of the press; none of these liberties were
thought compatible with a well-ordered state,
until they had proved their possibility by actually existing as facts. That an institution or a
practice is customary is no presumption of its
goodness, when any other sufficient cause can be

12

assigned for its existence. There is no difficulty
in understanding why the subjection of women
has been a custom. No other explanation is
needed than physical force.

That those who were physically weaker should
have been made legally inferior, is quite conformable to the mode in which the world has
been governed. Until very lately, the rule of
physical strength was the general law of human
affairs. Throughout history, the nations, races,
classes, which found themselves the strongest,
either in muscles, in riches, or in military discipline, have conquered and held in subjection the
rest. If, even in the most improved nations, the
law of the sword is at last discountenanced as
unworthy, it is only since the calumniated
eighteenth century. Wars of conquest have only
ceased since democratic revolutions began. The
world is very young, and has but just begun to
cast off injustice. It is only now getting rid of
negro slavery. It is only now getting rid of
monarchical despotism. It is only now getting
rid of hereditary feudal nobility. It is only now
getting rid of disabilities on the ground of
religion. It is only beginning to treat any *men* as
citizens, except the rich and a favoured portion
of the middle class. Can we wonder that it has
not yet done as much for women? As society was
constituted until the last few generations, inequality was its very basis; association grounded
on equal rights scarcely existed; to be equals was
to be enemies; two persons could hardly co-
operate in anything, or meet in any amicable

relation, without the law's appointing that one
of them should be the superior of the other. Mankind have outgrown this state, and all things now
tend to substitute, as the general principle of
human relations, a just equality, instead of the
dominion of the strongest. But of all relations,
that between men and women being the nearest
and most intimate, and connected with the
greatest number of strong emotions, was sure to
be the last to throw off the old rule and receive
the new: for in proportion to the strength of a
feeling, is the tenacity with which it clings to the
forms and circumstances with which it has even
accidentally become associated.

When a prejudice, which has any hold on the
feelings, finds itself reduced to the unpleasant
necessity of assigning reasons, it thinks it has
done enough when it has re-asserted the very
point in dispute, in phrases which appeal to the
pre-existing feeling. Thus, many persons think
they have sufficiently justified the restrictions on
women's field of action, when they have said that
the pursuits from which women are excluded are
unfeminine, and that the *proper sphere* of women
is not politics or publicity, but private and
domestic life.

We deny the right of any portion of the species
to decide for another portion, or any individual
for another individual, what is and what is not
their "proper sphere." The proper sphere for all
human beings is the largest and highest which
they are able to attain to. What this is, cannot be
ascertained, without complete liberty of choice.

The speakers at the Convention in America have therefore done wisely and right, in refusing to entertain the question of the peculiar aptitudes either of women or of men, or the limits within this or that occupation may be supposed to be more adapted to the one or to the other. They justly maintain, that these questions can only be satisfactorily answered by perfect freedom. Let every occupation be open to all, without favour or discouragement to any, and employments will fall into the hands of those men or women who are found by experience to be most capable of worthily exercising them. There need be no fear that women will take out of the hands of men any occupation which men perform better than they. Each individual will prove his or her capacities, in the only way in which capacities can be proved—by trial; and the world will have the benefit of the best faculties of all its inhabitants. But to interfere beforehand by an arbitrary limit, and declare that whatever be the genius, talent, energy, or force of mind of an individual of a certain sex or class, those faculties shall not be exerted, or shall be exerted only in some few of the many modes in which others are permitted to use theirs, is not only an injustice to the individual, and a detriment to society, which loses what it can ill spare, but is also the most effectual mode of providing that, in the sex or class so fettered, the qualities which are not permitted to be exercised shall not exist.

We shall follow the very proper example of the Convention, in not entering into the question of

the alleged differences in physical or mental
qualities between the sexes; not because we have
nothing to say, but because we have too much;
to discuss this one point tolerably would need all
the space we have to bestow on the entire subject.* But if those who assert that the "proper
sphere" for women is the domestic, mean by this
that they have not shown themselves qualified
for any other, the assertion evinces great ignorance of life and of history. Women have
shown fitness for the highest social functions,
exactly in proportion as they have been admitted
to them. By a curious anomaly, though in-
eligible to even the lowest offices of State, they

* An excellent passage on this part of the subject, from one
of Sydney Smith's contributions to the Edinburgh Review,
we will not refrain from quoting: "A great deal has been
said of the original difference of capacity between men and
women, as if women were more quick and men more
judicious—as if women were more remarkable for delicacy
of association, and men for stronger powers of attention.
All this, we confess, appears to us very fanciful. That there
is a difference in the understandings of the men and the
women we every day meet with, everybody, we suppose,
must perceive; but there is none surely which may not be
accounted for by the difference of circumstances in which
they have been placed, without referring to any con-
jectural difference of original conformation of mind. As
long as boys and girls run about in the dirt, and trundle
hoops together, they are both precisely alike. If you catch
up one-half of these creatures, and train them to a particular set of actions and opinions, and the other half to a
perfectly opposite set, of course their understandings will
differ, as one or the other sort of occupations has called this
or that talent into action. There is surely no occasion to go
into any deeper or more abstruse reasoning, in order to
explain so very simple a phenomenon." (*Sydney Smith's
Works*, vol. i, p. 200.)

are in some countries admitted to the highest of
all, the regal; and if there is any one function for
which they have shown a decided vocation, it is
that of reigning. Not to go back to ancient
history, we look in vain for abler or firmer rulers
than Elizabeth; than Isabella of Castile; than
Maria Teresa; than Catherine of Russia; than
Blanche, mother of Louis IX of France;
than Jeanne d'Albret, mother of Henri Quatre.
There are few kings on record who contended with
more difficult circumstances, or overcame them
more triumphantly, than these. Even in semi-
barbarous Asia, princesses who have never been
seen by men, other than those of their own
family, or ever spoken with them unless from
behind a curtain, have as regents, during the
minority of their sons, exhibited many of the
most brilliant examples of just and vigorous administration. In the middle ages, when the
distance between the upper and lower ranks was
greater than even between women and men, and
the women of the privileged class, however
subject to tyranny from the men of the same
class, were at a less distance below them than
any one else was, and often in their absence
represented them in their functions and authority—numbers of heroic châtelaines, like Jeanne
de Montfort, or the great Countess of Derby as
late even as the time of Charles I, distinguished
themselves not only by their political but their
military capacity. In the centuries immediately
before and after the Reformation, ladies of royal
houses, as diplomatists, as governors of provinces,

or as the confidential advisers of kings, equalled
the first statesmen of their time: and the treaty
of Cambray, which gave peace to Europe,
was negotiated in conferences where no other
person was present, by the aunt of the Emperor
Charles the Fifth, and the mother of Francis the
First.

Concerning the fitness, then, of women for
politics, there can be no question: but the
dispute is more likely to turn upon the fitness of
politics for women. When the reasons alleged for
excluding women from active life in all its higher
departments are stripped of their garb of declamatory phrases, and reduced to the simple
expression of a meaning, they seem to be
mainly three: first, the incompatibility of active
life with maternity, and with the cares of a
household; secondly, its alleged hardening effect
on the character; and thirdly, the inexpediency
of making an addition to the already excessive
pressure of competition in every kind of professional or lucrative employment.

The first, the maternity argument, is usually
laid most stress upon: although (it needs hardly
be said) this reason, if it be one, can apply only
to mothers. It is neither necessary nor just to
make imperative on women that they shall be
either mothers or nothing; or that if they have
been mothers once, they shall be nothing else
during the whole remainder of their lives.
Neither women nor men need any law to exclude
them from an occupation, if they have undertaken another which is incompatible with it. No

one proposes to exclude the male sex from Parliament because a man may be a soldier or sailor in active service, or a merchant whose business requires all his time and energies. Nine-tenths of the occupations of men exclude them *de facto* from public life, as effectually as if they were excluded by law; but that is no reason for making laws to exclude even the nine-tenths, much less the remaining tenth. The reason of the case is the same for women as for men. There is no need to make provision by law that a woman shall not carry on the active details of a household, or of the education of children, and at the same time practice a profession, or be elected to parliament Where incompatibility is real, it will take care of itself: but there is gross injustice in making the incompatibility a pretence for the exclusion of those in whose case it does not exist. And these, if they were free to choose, would be a very large proportion. The maternity argument deserts its supporters in the case of single women, a large and increasing class of the population; a fact which, it is not irrelevant to remark, by tending to diminish the excessive competition of numbers, is calculated to assist greatly the prosperity of all. There is no inherent reason or necessity that all women should voluntarily choose to devote their lives to one animal function and its consequences. Numbers of women are wives and mothers only because there is no other career open to them, no other occupation for their feelings or their activities. Every improvement in their education, and enlargement of their faculties, everything which renders them more qualified for any other mode of life, increases the number of those to whom it is an injury and an oppression to be denied the choice. To say that women must be excluded from active life because maternity disqualifies them for it, is in fact to say, that every other career should be forbidden them in order that maternity may be their only resource.

But secondly, it is urged, that to give the same freedom of occupation to women as to men, would be an injurious addition to the crowd of competitors, by whom the avenues to almost all kinds of employment are choked up, and its remuneration depressed. This argument, it is to be observed, does not reach the political question. It gives no excuse for withholding from women the rights of citizenship. The suffrage, the jury-box, admission to the legislature and to office, it does not touch. It bears only on the industrial branch of the subject. Allowing it, then, in an economical point of view, its full force; assuming that to lay open to women the employments now monopolized by men, would tend, like the breaking down of other monopolies, to lower the rate of remuneration in those employments; let us consider what is the amount of this evil consequence, and what the compensation for it. The worst ever asserted, much worse than is at all likely to be realized, is that if women competed with men, a man and a woman could not together earn more than is now earned by the man alone. Let us make this supposition, the most unfavourable supposition possible: the joint income of the two would be the same as before, while the woman would be raised from the position of a servant to that of a partner. Even if every woman, as matters now stand, had a claim on some man for support, how infinitely preferable is it that part of the income should be of the woman's earning, even if the aggregate sum were but little increased by it, rather than that she should be compelled to stand aside in order that men may be the sole earners, and the sole dispensers of what is earned. Even under the present laws respecting the property of women, a woman who contributes materially to the support of the family, cannot be treated in the same contemptuously tyrannical manner as one who, however she may toil as a domestic drudge, is a dependent on the man for subsistence.* As for the depression of wages by increase of competition, remedies will be found for it in time. Palliatives might be applied immediately; for instance, a more rigid exclusion of children from industrial employment, during the years in which they ought to be working only to strengthen their bodies and minds for after-life. Children are necessarily dependent, and under

* The truly horrible effects of the present state of the law among the lowest of the working population, is exhibited in those cases of hideous maltreatment of their wives by working men, with which every newspaper, every police report, teems. Wretches unfit to have the smallest authority over any living thing, have a helpless woman for their household slave. These excesses could not exist if women both earned, and had the right to possess, a part of the income of the family.

the power of others; and their labour, being not
for themselves but for the gain of their parents, is
a proper subject for legislative regulation. With
respect to the future, we neither believe that
improvident multiplication, and the consequent
excessive difficulty of gaining a subsistence, will
always continue, nor that the division of mankind into capitalists and hired labourers, and
the regulation of the reward of labourers mainly
by demand and supply, will be for ever, or even
much longer, the rule of the world. But so long as
competition is the general law of human life, it is
tyranny to shut out one-half of the competitors.
All who have attained the age of self-govern-
ment have an equal claim to be permitted to sell
whatever kind of useful labour they are capable
of, for the price which it will bring.

The third objection to the admission of
women to political or professional life, its alleged
hardening tendency, belongs to an age now past,
and is scarcely to be comprehended by people of
the present time. There are still, however,
persons who say that the world and its avocations
render men selfish and unfeeling; that the
struggles, rivalries, and collisions of business and
of politics make them harsh and unamiable; that
if half the species must unavoidably be given up
to these things, it is the more necessary that the
other half should be kept free from them; that
to preserve women from the bad influences of
the world, is the only chance of preventing men
from being wholly given up to them.

There would have been plausibility in this

argument when the world was still in the age of violence; when life was full of physical conflict, and every man had to redress his injuries or those of others, by the sword or by the strength of his arm. Women, like priests, by being exempted from such responsibilities, and from some part of the accompanying dangers, may have been enabled to exercise a beneficial influence. But in the present condition of human life, we do not know where those hardening influences are to be found, to which men are subject and from which women are at present exempt. Individuals now-a-days are seldom called upon to fight hand to hand, even with peaceful weapons; personal enmities and rivalities count for little in worldly transactions; the general pressure of circumstances, not the adverse will of individuals, is the obstacle men now have to make head against. That pressure, when excessive, breaks the spirit, and cramps and sours the feelings, but not less of women than of men, since they suffer certainly not less from its evils. There are still quarrels and dislikes, but the sources of them are changed. The feudal chief once found his bitterest enemy in his powerful neighbour, the minister or courtier in his rival for place: but opposition of interest in active life, as a cause of personal animosity, is out of date; the enmities of the present day arise not from great things but small, from what people say of one another, more than from what they do; and if there are hatred, malice, and all uncharitableness, they are to be found among women fully as much as among men. In the present state of civilization, the notion of guarding women from the hardening influences of the world, could only be realized by secluding them from society altogether. The common duties of common life, as at present constituted, are incompatible with any other softness in women than weakness. Surely weak minds in weak bodies must ere long cease to be even supposed to be either attractive or amiable.

But, in truth, none of these arguments and considerations touch the foundations of the subject. The real question is, whether it is right and expedient that one-half of the human race should pass through life in a state of forced subordination to the other half. If the best state of human society is that of being divided into two parts, one consisting of persons with a will and a substantive existence, the other of humble companions to these persons, attached, each of them to one, for the purpose of bringing up *his* children, and making *his* home pleasant to him; if this is the place assigned to women, it is but kindness to educate them for this; to make them believe that the greatest good fortune which can befal them, is to be chosen by some man for this purpose; and that every other career which the world deems happy or honourable, is closed to them by the law, not of social institutions, but of nature and destiny.

When, however, we ask why the existence of one-half the species should be merely ancillary to that of the other—why each woman should be a mere appendage to a man, allowed to have no interests of her own, that there may be nothing to compete in her mind with his interests and his pleasure; the only reason which can be given is, that men like it. It is agreeable to them that men should live for their own sake, women for the sake of men: and the qualities and conduct in subjects which are agreeable to rulers, they succeed for a long time in making the subjects themselves consider as their appropriate virtues. Helvetius has met with much obloquy for asserting, that persons usually mean by virtues the qualities which are useful or convenient to themselves. How truly this is said of mankind in general, and how wonderfully the ideas of virtue set afloat by the powerful, are caught and imbibed by those under their dominion, is exemplified by the manner in which the world were once persuaded that the supreme virtue of subjects was loyalty to kings, and are still persuaded that the paramount virtue of womanhood is loyalty to men. Under a nominal recognition of a moral code common to both, in practice self-will and self-assertion form the type of what are designated as manly virtues, while abnegation of self, patience, resignation, and submission to power, unless when resistance is commanded by other interests than their own, have been stamped by general consent as pre-eminently the duties and graces required of women. The meaning being merely, that power makes itself the centre of moral obligation, and that a man likes to have his own will, but does not like that his domestic companion should have a will different from his.

We are far from pretending that in modern and civilized times, no reciprocity of obligation is acknowledged on the part of the stronger. Such an assertion would be very wide of the truth. But even this reciprocity, which has disarmed tyranny, at least in the higher and middle classes, of its most revolting features, yet when combined with the original evil of the dependent condition of women, has introduced in its turn serious evils.

In the beginning, and among tribes which are still in a primitive condition, women were and are the slaves of men for purposes of toil. All the hard bodily labour devolves on them. The Australian savage is idle, while women painfully dig up the roots on which he lives. An American Indian, when he has killed a deer, leaves it, and sends a woman to carry it home. In a state somewhat more advanced, as in Asia, women were and are the slaves of men for purposes of sensuality. In Europe there early succeeded a third and milder dominion, secured not by blows, nor by locks and bars, but by sedulous inculcation on the mind; feelings also of kindness, and ideas of duty, such as a superior owes to inferiors under his protection, became more and more involved in the relation. But it did not, for many ages, become a relation of companionship, even between unequals. The lives of the two persons were apart. The wife was part of the furniture of home—of the resting-place to which the man

returned from business or pleasure. His occupations were, as they still are, among men; his
pleasures and excitements also were, for the
most part, among men—among his equals. He
was a patriarch and a despot within four walls,
and irresponsible power had its effect, greater or
less according to his disposition, in rendering him
domineering, exacting, self-worshipping, when
not capriciously or brutally tyrannical. But if
the moral part of his nature suffered, it was not
necessarily so, in the same degree, with the
intellectual or the active portion. He might have
as much vigour of mind and energy of character
as his nature enabled him, and as the circumstances of his times allowed. He might write the
Paradise Lost, or win the battle of Marengo. This
was the condition of the Greeks and Romans,
and of the moderns until a recent date. Their
relations with their domestic subordinates
occupied a mere corner, though a cherished one,
of their lives. Their education as men, the
formation of their character and faculties, depended mainly on a different class of influences.

It is otherwise now. The progress of improvement has imposed on all possessors of power, and
of domestic power among the rest, an increased
and increasing sense of correlative obligation.
No man now thinks that his wife has no claim
upon his actions but such as he may accord to
her. All men of any conscience believe that their
duty to their wives is one of the most binding of
their obligations. Nor is it supposed to consist
solely in protection, which, in the present state of

civilization, women have almost ceased to need:
it involves care for their happiness and consideration of their wishes, with a not unfrequent
sacrifice of their own to them. The power of
husbands has reached the stage which the power
of kings had arrived at, when opinion did not
yet question the rightfulness of arbitrary power,
but in theory, and to a certain extent in practice,
condemned the selfish use of it. This improvement in the moral sentiments of mankind, and
increased sense of the consideration due by every
man to those who have no one but himself to
look to, has tended to make home more and more
the centre of interest, and domestic circumstances and society a larger and larger part of
life, and of its pursuits and pleasures. The
tendency has been strengthened by the changes
of tastes and manners which have so remarkably
distinguished the last two or three generations.
In days not far distant, men found their excitement and filled up their time in violent bodily
exercises, noisy merriment, and intemperance.
They have now, in all but the very poorest
classes, lost their inclination for these things,
and for the coarser pleasures generally; they
have now scarcely any tastes but those which
they have in common with women, and, for the
first time in the world, men and women are
really companions. A most beneficial change, if
the companionship were between equals; but
being between unequals, it produces, what good
observers have noticed, though without per-
ceiving its cause, a progressive deterioration

among men in what had hitherto been considered the masculine excellences. Those who are so careful that women should not become men, do not see that men are becoming, what they have decided that women should be—are falling into the feebleness which they have so long cultivated in their companions. Those who are associated in their lives, tend to become assimilated in character. In the present closeness of association between the sexes, men cannot retain manliness unless women acquire it.

There is hardly any situation more unfavourable to the maintenance of elevation of character or force of intellect, than to live in the society, and seek by preference the sympathy, of inferiors in mental endowments. Why is it that we constantly see in life so much of intellectual and moral promise followed by such inadequate performance, but because the aspirant has compared himself only with those below himself, and has not sought improvement or stimulus from measuring himself with his equals or superiors. In the present state of social life, this is becoming the general condition of men. They care less and less for any sympathies, and are less and less under any personal influences, but those of the domestic roof. Not to be misunderstood, it is necessary that we should distinctly disclaim the belief, that women are even now inferior in intellect to men. There are women who are the equals in intellect of any men who ever lived; and comparing ordinary women with ordinary men, the varied though petty details which

compose the occupation of most women, call
forth probably as much of mental ability, as the
uniform routine of the pursuits which are the
habitual occupation of a large majority of men.
It is from nothing in the faculties themselves,
but from the petty subjects and interests on
which alone they are exercised, that the companionship of women, such as their present
circumstances make them, so often exercises a
dissolvent influence on high faculties and aspirations in men. If one of the two has no knowledge
and no care about the great ideas and purposes
which dignify life, or about any of its practical
concerns save personal interests and personal
vanities, her conscious, and still more her unconscious influence, will, except in rare cases,
reduce to a secondary place in his mind, if not
entirely extinguish, those interests which she
cannot or does not share.

Our argument here brings us into collision
with what may be termed the moderate re-
formers of the education of women; a sort of
persons who cross the path of improvement on
all great questions; those who would maintain
the old bad principles, mitigating their consequences. These say, that women should be, not
slaves, nor servants, but companions; and educated for that office (they do not say that men
should be educated to be the companions of
women). But since uncultivated women are not
suitable companions for cultivated men, and a
man who feels interest in things above and
beyond the family circle wishes that his com-

panion should sympathize with him in that interest; they therefore say, let women improve their understanding and taste, acquire general knowledge, cultivate poetry, art, even coquet with science, and some stretch their liberality so far as to say, inform themselves on politics; not as pursuits, but sufficiently to feel an interest in the subjects, and to be capable of holding a conversation on them with the husband, or at least of understanding and imbibing his wisdom. Very agreeable to him, no doubt, but unfortunately the reverse of improving. It is from having intellectual communion only with those to whom they can lay down the law, that so few men continue to advance in wisdom beyond the first stages. The most eminent men cease to improve, if they associate only with disciples. When they have overtopped those who immediately surround them, if they wish for further growth, they must seek for others of their own stature to consort with. The mental companionship which is improving, is communion between active minds, not mere contact between an active mind and a passive. This inestimable advantage is even now enjoyed, when a strong-minded man and a strong-minded woman are, by a rare chance, united: and would be had far oftener, if education took the same pains to form strong-minded women which it takes to prevent them from being formed. The modern, and what are regarded as the improved and enlightened modes of education of women, abjure, as far as words go, an education of mere show, and profess to aim at solid instruction, but mean by that expression, superficial information on solid subjects. Except accomplishments, which are now generally regarded as to be taught well if taught at all, nothing is taught to women thoroughly. Small portions only of what it is attempted to teach thoroughly to boys, are the whole of what it is intended or desired to teach to women. What makes intelligent beings is the power of thought: the stimuli which call forth that power are the interest and dignity of thought itself, and a field for its practical application. Both motives are cut off from those who are told from infancy that thought, and all its greater applications, are other people's business, while theirs is to make themselves agreeable to other people. High mental powers in women will be but an exceptional accident, until every career is open to them, and until they, as well as men, are educated for themselves and for the world—not one sex for the other.

In what we have said on the effect of the inferior position of women, combined with the present constitution of married life, we have thus far had in view only the most favourable cases, those in which there is some real approach to that union and blending of characters and of lives, which the theory of the relation contemplates as its ideal standard. But if we look to the great majority of cases, the effect of womens' legal inferiority, on the character both of women and of men, must be painted in far darker colours. We do not speak here of the

grosser brutalities, nor of the man's power to
seize on the woman's earnings, or compel her to
live with him against her will. We do not address
ourselves to any one who requires to have it
proved that these things should be remedied. We
suppose average cases, in which there is neither
complete union nor complete disunion of feelings
and character; and we affirm that in such cases
the influence of the dependence on the woman's
side, is demoralizing to the character of both.

The common opinion is, that whatever may be
the case with the intellectual, the moral influence of women over men is almost salutary.
It is, we are often told, the great counteractive
of selfishness. However the case may be as to
personal influence, the influence of the position
tends eminently to promote selfishness. The
most insignificant of men, the man who can
obtain influence or consideration nowhere else,
finds one place where he is chief and head. There
is one person, often greatly his superior in understanding, who is obliged to consult him, and
whom he is not obliged to consult. He is judge,
magistrate, ruler, over their joint concerns;
arbiter of all differences between them. The
justice or conscience to which her appeal must
be made, is his justice and conscience: it is his
to hold the balance and adjust the scales between
his own claims or wishes and those of another.
His is now the only tribunal, in civilized life, in
which the same person is judge and party. A
generous mind, in such a situation, makes the
balance incline against his own side, and gives

the other not less, but more, than a fair equality; and thus the weaker side may be enabled to turn the very fact of dependence into an instrument of power, and in default of justice, take an ungenerous advantage of generosity; rendering the unjust power, to those who make an unselfish use of it, a torment and a burthen. But how is it when average men are invested with this power, without reciprocity and without responsibility? Give such a man the idea that he is first in law and in opinion—that to will is his part, and hers to submit; it is absurd to suppose that this idea merely glides over his mind, without sinking into it, or having any effect on his feelings and practice. The propensity to make himself the first object of consideration, and others at most the second, is not so rare as to be wanting where everything seems purposely arranged for encouraging its indulgence. If there is any self-will in the man, he becomes either the conscious or unconscious despot of his household. The wife, indeed, often succeeds in gaining her objects, but it is by some of the many various forms of indirectness and management.

Thus the position is corrupting equally to both; in the one it produces the vices of power, in the other those of artifice. Women, in their present physical and moral state, having stronger impulses, would naturally be franker and more direct than men; yet all the old saws and traditions represent them as artful and dissembling. Why? Because their only way to their objects is by indirect paths. In all countries

where women have strong wishes and active
minds, this consequence is inevitable: and if it is
less conspicuous in England than in some other
places, it is because Englishwomen, saving
occasional exceptions, have ceased to have either
strong wishes or active minds.

We are not now speaking of cases in which
there is anything deserving the name of strong
affection on both sides. That, where it exists, is
too powerful a principle not to modify greatly
the bad influences of the situation; it seldom,
however, destroys them entirely. Much oftener
the bad influences are too strong for the affection,
and destroy it. The highest order of durable and
happy attachments would be a hundred times
more frequent than they are, if the affection
which the two sexes sought from one another
were that genuine friendship, which only exists
between equals in privileges as in faculties. But
with regard to what is commonly called affection
in married life—the habitual and almost
mechanical feeling of kindliness, and pleasure in
each other's society, which generally grows up
between persons who constantly live together,
unless there is actual dislike—there is nothing in
this to contradict or qualify the mischievous influence of the unequal relation. Such feelings
often exist between a sultan and his favourites,
between a master and his servants; they are
merely examples of the pliability of human
nature, which accommodates itself in some
degree even to the worst circumstances, and
the commonest natures always the most easily.

With respect to the influence personally
exercised by women over men, it, no doubt,
renders them less harsh and brutal; in ruder
times, it was often the only softening influence to
which they were accessible. But the assertion,
that the wife's influence renders the man less
selfish, contains, as things now are, fully as much
error as truth. Selfishness towards the wife herself, and towards those in whom she is interested,
the children, though favoured by her dependence, the wife's influence, no doubt, tends to
counteract. But the general effect on him of her
character, so long as her interests are concen-
trated in the family, tends but to substitute for
individual selfishness a family selfishness, wearing an amiable guise, and putting on the mask of
duty. How rarely is the wife's influence on the
side of public virtue; how rarely does it do otherwise than discourage any effort of principle by
which the private interests or worldly vanities of
the family can be expected to suffer. Public
spirit, sense of duty towards the public good, is
of all virtues, as women are now educated and
situated, the most rarely to be found among
them; they have seldom even, what in men is
often a partial substitute for public spirit, a
sense of personal honour connected with any
public duty. Many a man, whom no money or
personal flattery would have bought, has
bartered his political opinions against a title or
invitations for his wife; and a still greater
number are made mere hunters after the puerile
vanities of society, because their wives value

them. As for opinions; in Catholic countries, the wife's influence is another name for that of the priest; he gives her, in the hopes and emotions connected with a future life, a consolation for the sufferings and disappointments which are her ordinary lot in this. Elsewhere, her weight is thrown into the scale either of the most commonplace, or of the most outwardly prosperous opinions: either those by which censure will be escaped, or by which worldly advancement is likeliest to be procured. In England, the wife's influence is usually on the illiberal and anti-popular side: this is generally the gaining side for personal interest and vanity; and what to her is the democracy or liberalism in which she has no part—which leaves her the Pariah it found her? The man himself, when he marries, usually declines into Conservatism; begins to sympathize with the holders of power, more than with its victims, and thinks it his part to be on the side of authority. As to mental progress, except those vulgar attainments by which vanity or ambition are promoted, there is generally an end to it in a man who marries a woman mentally his inferior; unless, indeed, he is unhappy in marriage, or becomes indifferent. From a man of twenty-five or thirty, after he is married, an experienced observer seldom expects any further progress in mind or feelings. It is rare that the progress already made is maintained. Any spark of the *mens divinior* which might otherwise have spread and become a flame, seldom survives for any length of time unextinguished. For a mind which learns to be satisfied with what it already is—which does not incessantly look forward to a degree of improvement not yet reached—becomes relaxed, self-indulgent, and loses the spring and the tension which maintain it even at the point already attained. And there is no fact in human nature to which experience bears more invariable testimony than to this—that all social or sympathetic influences which do not raise up, pull down; if they do not tend to stimulate and exalt the mind, they tend to vulgarize it.

For the interest, therefore, not only of women but of men, and of human improvement in the widest sense, the emancipation of women, which the modern world often boasts of having effected, and for which credit is sometimes given to civilization, and sometimes to Christianity, cannot stop where it is. If it were either necessary or just that one portion of mankind should remain mentally and spiritually only half developed, the development of the other portion ought to have been made, as far as possible, independent of their influence. Instead of this, they have become the most intimate, and it may now be said, the only intimate associates of those to whom yet they are sedulously kept inferior; and have been raised just high enough to drag the others down to themselves.

We have left behind a host of vulgar objections either as not worthy of an answer, or as answered by the general course of our remarks. A few words, however, must be said on one plea, which in England is made much use of for giving an unselfish air to the upholding of selfish privileges, and which, with unobserving, unreflecting people, passes for much more than it is worth. Women, it is said, do not desire—do not seek, what is called their emancipation. On the contrary, they generally disown such claims when made in their behalf, and fall with *acharnement* upon any one of themselves who identifies herself with their common cause.

Supposing the fact to be true in the fullest extent ever asserted, if it proves that European women ought to remain as they are, it proves exactly the same with respect to Asiatic women; for they too, instead of murmuring at their seclusion, and at the restraint imposed upon them, pride themselves on it, and are astonished at the effrontery of women who receive visits from male acquaintances, and are seen in the streets unveiled. Habits of submission make men as well as women servile-minded. The vast population of Asia do not desire or value, probably would not accept, political liberty, nor the savages of the forest, civilization; which does not prove that either of those things is undesirable for them, or that they will not, at some future time, enjoy it. Custom hardens human beings to any kind of degradation, by deadening the part of their nature which would resist it. And the case of women is, in this respect, even a peculiar one, for no other inferior caste that we have heard of have been taught to regard their degradation as their honour. The argument, however, implies a secret consciousness that the

alleged preference of women for their dependent
state is merely apparent, and arises from their
being allowed no choice; for if the preference be
natural, there can be no necessity for enforcing
it by law. To make laws compelling people to
follow their inclination, has not hitherto been
thought necessary by any legislator. The plea
that women do not desire any change, is the same
that has been urged, times out of mind, against
the proposal of abolishing any social evil—
"there is no complaint"; which is generally not
true, and when true, only so because there is not
that hope of success, without which complaint
seldom makes itself audible to unwilling ears.
How does the objector know that women do not
desire equality and freedom? He never knew a
woman who did not, or would not, desire it for
herself individually. It would be very simple to
suppose, that if they do desire it they will say so.
Their position is like that of the tenants or
labourers who vote against their own political
interests to please their landlords or employers; with the unique addition, that submission is inculcated on them from childhood, as
the peculiar attraction and grace of their
character. They are taught to think, that to
repel actively even an admitted injustice done
to themselves, is somewhat unfeminine, and had
better be left to some male friend or protector.
To be accused of rebelling against anything
which admits of being called an ordinance of
society, they are taught to regard as an imputa-
tion of a serious offence, to say the least, against

the proprieties of their sex. It requires unusual moral courage as well as disinterestedness in a woman, to express opinions favourable to women's enfranchisement, until, at least, there is some prospect of obtaining it. The comfort of her individual life, and her social consideration, usually depend on the good-will of those who hold the undue power, and to possessors of power any complaint, however bitter, of the misuse of it, is a less flagrant act of insubordination than to protest against the power itself. The professions of women in this matter remind us of the State offenders of old, who, on the point of execution, used to protest their love and devotion to the sovereign by whose unjust mandate they suffered. Griselda herself might be matched from the speeches put by Shakespeare into the mouths of male victims of kingly caprice and tyranny: the Duke of Buckingham, for example, in *Henry the Eighth*, and even Wolsey. The literary class of women, especially in England, are ostentatious in disclaiming the desire for equality or citizenship, and proclaiming their complete satisfaction with the place which society assigns to them; exercising in this, as in many other respects, a most noxious influence over the feelings and opinions of men, who unsuspectingly accept the servilities of toadyism as concessions to the force of truth, not considering that it is the personal interest of these women to profess whatever opinions they expect will be agreeable to men. It is not among men of talent, sprung from the people, and patronized and flattered by the aristocracy, that we look for the leaders of a democratic movement. Successful literary women are just as unlikely to prefer the cause of women to their own social consideration. They depend on men's opinion for their literary as well as for their feminine successes; and such is their bad opinion of men, that they believe there is not more than one in ten thousand who does not dislike and fear strength, sincerity, or high spirit in a woman. They are therefore anxious to earn pardon and toleration for whatever of these qualities their writings may exhibit on other subjects, by a studied display of submission on this: that they may give no occasion for vulgar men to say (what nothing will prevent vulgar men from saying), that learning makes women unfeminine, and that literary ladies are likely to be bad wives.

But enough of this; especially as the fact which affords the occasion for this notice, makes it impossible any longer to assert the universal acquiescence of women (saving individual exceptions) in their dependent condition. In the United States, at least, there are women, seemingly numerous, and now organized for action on the public mind, who demand equality in the fullest acceptation of the word, and demand it by a straightforward appeal to men's sense of justice, not plead for it with a timid deprecation of their displeasure.

Like other popular movements, however, this may be seriously retarded by the blunders of its adherents. Tried by the ordinary standard of public meetings, the speeches at the Convention are remarkable for the preponderance of the rational over the declamatory element; but there are some exceptions; and things to which it is impossible to attach any rational meaning, have found their way into the resolutions. Thus, the resolution which sets forth the claims made in behalf of women, after claiming equality in education, in industrial pursuits, and in political rights, enumerates as a fourth head of demand something under the name of "social and spiritual union," and "a medium of expressing the highest moral and spiritual views of justice," with other similar verbiage, serving only to mar the simplicity and rationality of the other demands; resembling those who would weakly attempt to combine nominal equality between men and women, with enforced distinctions in their privileges and functions. What is wanted for women is equal rights, equal admission to all social privileges; not a position apart, a sort of sentimental priesthood. To this, the only just and rational principle, both the resolutions and the speeches, for the most part, adhere. They contain so little which is akin to the nonsensical paragraph in question, that we suspect it not to be the work of the same hands as most of the other resolutions. The strength of the cause lies in the support of those who are influenced by reason and principle; and to attempt to recommend it by sentimentalities, absurd in reason, and inconsistent with the principle on which the movement is founded, is to place a good cause on a level with a bad one.

There are indications that the example of America will be followed on this side of the Atlantic; and the first step has been taken in that part of England where every serious movement in the direction of political progress has its commencement—the manufacturing districts of the North. On the 13th of February 1851, a petition of women, agreed to by a public meeting at Sheffield, and claiming the elective franchise, was presented to the House of Lords by the Earl of Carlisle.

THE
SUBJECTION OF WOMEN

CHAPTER I.

THE object of this Essay is to explain as
clearly as I am able, the grounds of an
opinion which I have held from the very earliest
period when I had formed any opinions at all on
social or political matters, and which, instead of
being weakened or modified, has been constantly
growing stronger by the progress of reflection
and the experience of life: That the principle
which regulates the existing social relations
between the two sexes—the legal subordination of
one sex to the other—is wrong in itself, and now
one of the chief hindrances to human improvement; and that it ought to be replaced by a
principle of perfect equality, admitting no power
or privilege on the one side, nor disability on the
other.

The very words necessary to express the task
I have undertaken, show how arduous it is.
But it would be a mistake to suppose that the
difficulty of the case must lie in the insufficiency
or obscurity of the grounds of reason on which

my conviction rests. The difficulty is that which exists in all cases in which there is a mass of feeling to be contended against. So long as an opinion is strongly rooted in the feelings, it gains rather than loses in stability by having a preponderating weight of argument against it. For if it were accepted as a result of argument, the refutation of the argument might shake the solidity of the conviction; but when it rests solely on feeling, the worse it fares in argumentative contest, the more persuaded its adherents are that their feeling must have some deeper ground, which the arguments do not reach; and while the feeling remains, it is always throwing up fresh intrenchments of argument to repair any breach made in the old. And there are so many causes tending to make the feelings connected with this subject the most intense and most deeply-rooted of all those which gather round and protect old institutions and customs, that we need not wonder to find them as yet less undermined and loosened than any of the rest by the progress of the great modern spiritual and social transition; nor suppose that the barbarisms to which men cling longest must be less barbarisms than those which they earlier shake off.

In every respect the burthen is hard on those who attack an almost universal opinion. They must be very fortunate as well as unusually capable if they obtain a hearing at all. They have more difficulty in obtaining a trial, than any other litigants have in getting a verdict. If they do extort a hearing, they are subjected to a set of logical requirements totally different from those exacted from other people. In all other cases, the burthen of proof is supposed to lie with the affirmative. If a person is charged with a murder, it rests with those who accuse him to give proof of his guilt, not with himself to prove his innocence. If there is a difference of opinion about the reality of any alleged historical event, in which the feelings of men in general are not much interested, as the Siege of Troy for example, those who maintain that the event took place are expected to produce their proofs, before those who take the other side can be required to say anything; and at no time are these required to do more than show that the evidence produced by the others is of no value. Again, in practical matters, the burthen of proof is supposed to be with those who are against liberty; who contend for any restriction or prohibition; either any limitation of the general freedom of human action, or any disqualification or disparity of privilege affecting one person or kind of persons, as compared with others. The *à priori* presumption is in favour of freedom and impartiality. It is held that there should be no restraint not required by the general good, and that the law should be no respecter of persons, but should treat all alike, save where dissimilarity of treatment is required by positive reasons, either of justice or of policy. But of none of these rules of evidence will the benefit be allowed to those who maintain the opinion I profess. It is useless for me to say that those who maintain the doctrine that men have a right to command and women are under an obligation to obey, or that men are fit for government and women unfit, are on the affirmative side of the question, and that they are bound to show positive evidence for the assertions, or submit to their rejection. It is equally unavailing for me to say that those who deny to women any freedom or privilege rightly allowed to men, having the double presumption against them that they are opposing freedom and recommending partiality, must be held to the strictest proof of their case, and unless their success be such as to exclude all doubt, the judgment ought to go against them. These would be thought good pleas in any common case; but they will not be thought so in this instance. Before I could hope to make any impression, I should be expected not only to answer all that has ever been said by those who take the other side of the question, but to imagine all that could be said by them—to find them in reasons, as well as answer all I find: and besides refuting all arguments for the affirmative, I shall be called upon for invincible positive arguments to prove a negative. And even if I could do all this, and leave the opposite party with a host of unanswered arguments against them, and not a single unrefuted one on their side, I should be thought to have done little; for a cause supported on the one hand by universal usage, and on the other by so great a preponderance of popular sentiment, is supposed to have a presumption in its favour, superior to any conviction which an appeal to reason has power to produce in any intellects but those of a high class.

I do not mention these difficulties to complain of them; first, because it would be useless; they are inseparable from having to contend through people's understandings against the hostility of their feelings and practical tendencies: and truly the understandings of the majority of mankind would need to be much better cultivated than has ever yet been the case, before they can be asked to place such reliance in their own power of estimating arguments, as to give up practical principles in which they have been born and bred and which are the basis of much of the existing order of the world, at the first argumentative attack which they are not capable of logically resisting. I do not therefore quarrel with them for having too little faith in argument, but for having too much faith in custom and the general feeling. It is one of the characteristic prejudices of the reaction of the nineteenth century against the eighteenth, to accord to the unreasoning elements in human nature the infallibility which the eighteenth century is supposed to have ascribed to the reasoning elements. For the apotheosis of Reason we have substituted that of Instinct; and we call everything instinct which we find in ourselves and for which we cannot trace any rational foundation. This idolatry, infinitely more degrading than the other, and the most pernicious of the false worships of the present day, of all of which it is now the main support, will probably hold its ground until it gives way before a sound psychology, laying bare the real root of much that is bowed down to as the intention of Nature and the ordinance of God. As regards the present question, I am willing to accept the unfavourable conditions which the prejudice assigns to me. I consent that established custom, and the general feeling, should be deemed conclusive against me, unless that custom and feeling from age to age can be shown to have owed their existence to other causes than their soundness, and to have derived their power from the worse rather than the better parts of human nature. I am willing that judgment should go against me, unless I can show that my judge has been tampered with. The concession is not so great as it might appear; for to prove this, is by far the easiest portion of my task.

The generality of a practice is in some cases a strong presumption that it is, or at all events once was, conducive to laudable ends. This is the case, when the practice was first adopted, or afterwards kept up, as a means to such ends, and was grounded on experience of the mode in which they could be most effectually attained. If the authority of men over women, when first established, had been the result of a conscientious comparison between different modes of constituting the government of society; if, after trying various other modes of social organization—the government of women over men, equality between the two, and such mixed and divided modes of government as might be invented—it had been decided, on the testimony of experience, that the mode in which women are wholly under the rule of men, having no share at all in public concerns, and each in private being under the legal obligation of obedience to the man with whom she has associated her destiny, was the arrangement most conducive to the happiness and well being of both; its general adoption might then be fairly thought to be some evidence that, at the time when it was adopted, it was the best: though even then the considerations which recommended it may, like so many other primeval social facts of the greatest importance, have subsequently, in the course of ages, ceased to exist. But the state of the case is in every respect the reverse of this. In the first place, the opinion in favour of the present system, which entirely subordinates the weaker sex to the stronger, rests upon theory only; for there never has been trial made of any other : so that experience, in the sense in which it is vulgarly opposed to theory, cannot be pretended to have pronounced any verdict. And in the second place, the adoption of this system of inequality never was the result of deliberation, or forethought, or any social ideas, or any notion whatever of what conduced to the benefit of humanity or the good order of society. It arose simply from the fact that from the very earliest twilight of human society, every woman (owing to the value attached to her by men, combined with her inferiority in muscular strength) was found in a state of bondage to some man. Laws and systems of polity always begin by recognising the relations they find already exist-ing between individuals. They convert what was a mere physical fact into a legal right, give it the sanction of society, and principally aim at the substitution of public and organized means of asserting and protecting these rights, instead of the irregular and lawless conflict of physical strength. Those who had already been compelled to obedience became in this manner legally bound to it. Slavery, from being a mere affair of force between the master and the slave, became regularized and a matter of compact among the masters, who, binding themselves to one another for common protection, guaranteed by their collective strength the private possessions of each, including his slaves. In early times, the great majority of the male sex were slaves, as well as the whole of the female. And many ages elapsed, some of them ages of high cultivation, before any thinker was bold enough to question the rightfulness, and the absolute social necessity, either of the one slavery or of the other. By degrees such thinkers did arise: and (the general progress of society assisting) the slavery of the male sex has, in all the countries of Christian Europe at least (though, in one of them, only within the last few years) been at length abolished, and that of the female sex has been gradually changed into a milder form of dependence. But this dependence, as it exists at present, is not an original institution, taking a fresh start from considerations of justice and social expediency—it is the primitive state of slavery lasting on, through successive mitigations and modifications occasioned by the same causes which have softened the general manners, and brought all human relations more under the control of justice and the influence of humanity. It has not lost the taint of its brutal origin. No presumption in its favour, therefore, can be drawn from the fact of its existence. The only such presumption which it could be supposed to have, must be grounded on its having lasted till now, when so many other things which came down from the same odious source have been done away with. And this, indeed, is what makes it strange to ordinary ears, to hear it asserted that the inequality of rights between men and women has no other source than the law of the strongest.

That this statement should have the effect of a paradox, is in some respects creditable to the progress of civilization, and the improvement of the moral sentiments of mankind. We now live —that is to say, one or two of the most advanced nations of the world now live—in a state in which the law of the strongest seems to be entirely abandoned as the regulating principle of the world's affairs: nobody professes it, and, as regards most of the relations between human beings, nobody is permitted to practise it. When any one succeeds in doing so, it is under cover of some pretext which gives him the semblance of having some general social interest on his side.

This being the ostensible state of things, people flatter themselves that the rule of mere force is ended; that the law of the strongest cannot be the reason of existence of anything which has remained in full operation down to the present time. However any of our present institutions may have begun, it can only, they think, have been preserved to this period of advanced civilization by a well-grounded feeling of its adaptation to human nature, and conduciveness to the general good. They do not understand the great vitality and durability of institutions which place right on the side of might; how intensely they are clung to; how the good as well as the bad propensities and sentiments of those who have power in their hands, become identified with retaining it; how slowly these bad institutions give way, one at a time, the weakest first, beginning with those which are least interwoven with the daily habits of life; and how very rarely those who have obtained legal power because they first had physical, have ever lost their hold of it until the physical power had passed over to the other side. Such shifting of the physical force not having taken place in the case of women; this fact, combined with all the peculiar and characteristic features of the particular case, made it certain from the first that this branch of the system of right founded on might, though softened in its most atrocious features at an earlier period than several of the others, would be the very last to disappear. It was inevitable that this one case of a social relation grounded on force, would survive through generations of institutions grounded on equal justice, an almost solitary exception to the general character of their laws and customs; but which, so long as it does not proclaim its own origin, and as discussion has not brought out its true character, is not felt to jar with modern civilization, any more than domestic slavery among the Greeks jarred with their notion of themselves as a free people.

The truth is, that people of the present and the last two or three generations have lost all practical sense of the primitive condition of humanity; and only the few who have studied history accurately, or have much frequented the parts of the world occupied by the living representatives of ages long past, are able to form any mental picture of what society then was. People are not aware how entirely, in former ages, the law of superior strength was the rule of life; how publicly and openly it was avowed, I do not say cynically or shamelessly—for these words imply a feeling that there was something in it to be ashamed of, and no such notion could find a place in the faculties of any person in those ages, except a philosopher or a saint. History gives a cruel experience of human nature, in shewing how exactly the regard due to the life, possessions, and entire earthly happiness of any class of persons, was measured by what they had the power of enforcing; how all who made any resistance to authorities that had arms in their hands, however dreadful might be the provocation, had not only the law of force but all other laws, and all the notions of social obligation against them; and in the eyes of those whom they resisted, were not only guilty of crime, but of the worst of all crimes, deserving the most cruel chastisement which human beings could inflict. The first small vestige of a feeling of obligation in a superior to acknowledge any right in inferiors, began when he had been induced, for convenience, to make some promise to them. Though these promises, even when sanctioned by the most solemn oaths, were for many ages revoked or violated on the most trifling provocation or temptation, it is probable that this, except by persons of still worse than the average morality, was seldom done without some twinges of conscience. The ancient republics, being mostly grounded from the first upon some kind of mutual compact, or at any rate formed by an union of persons not very unequal in strength, afforded, in consequence, the first instance of a portion of human relations fenced round, and placed under the dominion of another law than

that of force. And though the original law of
force remained in full operation between them
and their slaves, and also (except so far as limited
by express compact) between a commonwealth
and its subjects, or other independent common-
wealths; the banishment of that primitive law
even from so narrow a field, commenced the regeneration of human nature, by giving birth to
sentiments of which experience soon demon-
strated the immense value even for material interests, and which thenceforward only required
to be enlarged, not created. Though slaves were
no part of the commonwealth, it was in the free
states that slaves were first felt to have rights as
human beings. The Stoics were, I believe, the
first (except so far as the Jewish law constitutes
an exception) who taught as a part of morality
that men were bound by moral obligations to
their slaves. No one, after Christianity became
ascendant, could ever again have been a stranger
to this belief, in theory ; nor, after the rise of the
Catholic Church, was it ever without persons to
stand up for it. Yet to enforce it was the most
arduous task which Christianity ever had to perform. For more than a thousand years the
Church kept up the contest, with hardly any per-
ceptible success. It was not for want of power
over men's minds. Its power was prodigious.
It could make kings and nobles resign their most

valued possessions to enrich the Church. It could make thousands, in the prime of life and the height of worldly advantages, shut themselves up in convents to work out their salvation by poverty, fasting, and prayer. It could send hundreds of thousands across land and sea, Europe and Asia, to give their lives for the deliverance of the Holy Sepulchre. It could make kings relinquish wives who were the object of their passionate attachment, because the Church declared that they were within the seventh (by our calculation the fourteenth) degree of relationship. All this it did; but it could not make men fight less with one another, nor tyrannize less cruelly over the serfs, and when they were able, over burgesses. It could not make them renounce either of the applications of force; force militant, or force triumphant. This they could never be induced to do until they were themselves in their turn compelled by superior force. Only by the growing power of kings was an end put to fighting except between kings, or competitors for kingship; only by the growth of a wealthy and warlike bourgeoisie in the fortified towns, and of a plebeian infantry which proved more powerful in the field than the undisciplined chivalry, was the insolent tyranny of the nobles over the bourgeoisie and peasantry brought within some bounds. It was persisted in not only until, but long after, the oppressed had obtained a power enabling them often to take conspicuous vengeance; and on the Continent much of it continued to the time of the French Revolution, though in England the earlier and better organization of the democratic classes put an end to it sooner, by establishing equal laws and free national institutions.

If people are mostly so little aware how completely, during the greater part of the duration of our species, the law of force was the avowed rule of general conduct, any other being only a special and exceptional consequence of peculiar ties—and from how very recent a date it is that the affairs of society in general have been even pretended to be regulated according to any moral law; as little do people remember or consider, how institutions and customs which never had any ground but the law of force, last on into ages and states of general opinion which never would have permitted their first establishment. Less than forty years ago, Englishmen might still by law hold human beings in bondage as saleable property : within the present century they might kidnap them and carry them off, and work them literally to death. This absolutely extreme case of the law of force, condemned by those who can tolerate almost every other form of arbitrary power, and which, of all others, presents features the most revolting to the feelings

of all who look at it from an impartial position,
was the law of civilized and Christian England
within the memory of persons now living : and
in one half of Anglo-Saxon America three or
four years ago, not only did slavery exist, but
the slave trade, and the breeding of slaves ex-
pressly for it, was a general practice between
slave states. Yet not only was there a greater
strength of sentiment against it, but, in England
at least, a less amount either of feeling or of interest in favour of it, than of any other of the
customary abuses of force : for its motive was
the love of gain, unmixed and undisguised ; and
those who profited by it were a very small nu-
merical fraction of the country, while the natural
feeling of all who were not personally interested
in it, was unmitigated abhorrence. So extreme
an instance makes it almost superfluous to refer
to any other : but consider the long duration of
absolute monarchy. In England at present it
is the almost universal conviction that military
despotism is a case of the law of force, having
no other origin or justification. Yet in all the
great nations of Europe except England it either
still exists, or has only just ceased to exist, and
has even now a strong party favourable to it in
all ranks of the people, especially among persons
of station and consequence. Such is the power
of an established system, even when far from

universal; when not only in almost every period of history there have been great and well-known examples of the contrary system, but these have almost invariably been afforded by the most illustrious and most prosperous communities. In this case, too, the possessor of the undue power, the person directly interested in it, is only one person, while those who are subject to it and suffer from it are literally all the rest. The yoke is naturally and necessarily humiliating to all persons, except the one who is on the throne, together with, at most, the one who expects to succeed to it. How different are these cases from that of the power of men over women! I am not now prejudging the question of its justifiableness. I am showing how vastly more permanent it could not but be, even if not justifiable, than these other dominations which have nevertheless lasted down to our own time. Whatever gratification of pride there is in the possession of power, and whatever personal interest in its exercise, is in this case 'not confined to a limited class, but common to the whole male sex. Instead of being, to most of its supporters, a thing desirable chiefly in the abstract, or, like the political ends usually contended for by factions, of little private importance to any but the leaders; it comes home to the person and hearth of every male head of a family, and of every one

who looks forward to being so. The clodhopper
exercises, or is to exercise, his share of the power
equally with the highest nobleman. And the
case is that in which the desire of power is the
strongest: for every one who desires power, desires
it most over those who are nearest to him, with
whom his life is passed, with whom he has most
concerns in common, and in whom any independence of his authority is oftenest likely to
interfere with his individual preferences. If, in
the other cases specified, powers manifestly
grounded only on force, and having so much less
to support them, are so slowly and with so much
difficulty got rid of, much more must it be so
with this, even if it rests on no better foundation
than those. We must consider, too, that the
possessors of the power have facilities in this
case, greater than in any other, to prevent any
uprising against it. Every one of the subjects
lives under the very eye, and almost, it may be
said, in the hands, of one of the masters—in
closer intimacy with him than with any of her
fellow-subjects ; with no means of combining
against him, no power of even locally over-
mastering him, and, on the other hand, with the
strongest motives for seeking his favour and
avoiding to give him offence. In struggles for
political emancipation, everybody knows how often
its champions are bought off by bribes, or daunted

by terrors. In the case of women, each individual of the subject-class is in a chronic state of bribery and intimidation combined. In setting up the standard of resistance, a large number of the leaders, and still more of the followers, must make an almost complete sacrifice of the pleasures or the alleviations of their own individual lot. If ever any system of privilege and enforced subjection had its yoke tightly riveted on the necks of those who are kept down by it, this has. I have not yet shown that it is a wrong system : but every one who is capable of thinking on the subject must see that even if it is, it was certain to outlast all other forms of unjust authority. And when some of the grossest of the other forms still exist in many civilized countries, and have only recently been got rid of in others, it would be strange if that which is so much the deepest-rooted had yet been perceptibly shaken anywhere. There is more reason to wonder that the protests and testimonies against it should have been so numerous and so weighty as they are.

Some will object, that a comparison cannot fairly be made between the government of the male sex and the forms of unjust power which I have adduced in illustration of it, since these are arbitrary, and the effect of mere usurpation, while it on the contrary is natural. But was

there ever any domination which did not appear
natural to those who possessed it? There was
a time when the division of mankind into two
classes, a small one of masters and a numerous
one of slaves, appeared, even to the most cultivated minds, to be a natural, and the only natural,
condition of the human race. No less an intellect, and one which contributed no less to the
progress of human thought, than Aristotle, held
this opinion without doubt or misgiving; and
rested it on the same premises on which the
same assertion in regard to the dominion of men
over women is usually based, namely that there
are different natures among mankind, free natures, and slave natures; that the Greeks were
of a free nature, the barbarian races of Thracians
and Asiatics of a slave nature. But why need I
go back to Aristotle? Did not the slaveowners
of the Southern United States maintain the same
doctrine, with all the fanaticism with which men
cling to the theories that justify their passions
and legitimate their personal interests? Did
they not call heaven and earth to witness that
the dominion of the white man over the black is
natural, that the black race is by nature incapable of freedom, and marked out for slavery?
some even going so far as to say that the freedom
of manual labourers is an unnatural order of
things anywhere. Again, the theorists of abso-

lute monarchy have always affirmed it to be the
only natural form of government; issuing from
the patriarchal, which was the primitive and
spontaneous form of society, framed on the
model of the paternal, which is anterior to society
itself, and, as they contend, the most natural
authority of all. Nay, for that matter, the law
of force itself, to those who could not plead any
other, has always seemed the most natural of all
grounds for the exercise of authority. Conquering races hold it to be Nature's own dictate that
the conquered should obey the conquerors, or, as
they euphoniously paraphrase it, that the feebler
and more unwarlike races should submit to the
braver and manlier. The smallest acquaintance
with human life in the middle ages, shows how
supremely natural the dominion of the feudal
nobility over men of low condition appeared to
the nobility themselves, and how unnatural the
conception seemed, of a person of the inferior
class claiming equality with them, or exercising
authority over them. It hardly seemed less so
to the class held in subjection. The emanci-
pated serfs and burgesses, even in their most
vigorous struggles, never made any pretension to
a share of authority; they only demanded more
or less of limitation to the power of tyrannizing
over them. So true is it that unnatural generally means only uncustomary, and that every-

thing which is usual appears natural. The subjection of women to men being a universal custom, any departure from it quite naturally appears unnatural. But how entirely, even in this case, the feeling is dependent on custom, appears by ample experience. Nothing so much astonishes the people of distant parts of the world, when they first learn anything about England, as to be told that it is under a queen: the thing seems to them so unnatural as to be almost incredible. To Englishmen this does not seem in the least degree unnatural, because they are used to it; but they do feel it unnatural that women should be soldiers or members of parliament. In the feudal ages, on the contrary, war and politics were not thought unnatural to women, because not unusual; it seemed natural that women of the privileged classes should be of manly character, inferior in nothing but bodily strength to their husbands and fathers. The independence of women seemed rather less unnatural to the Greeks than to other ancients, on account of the fabulous Amazons (whom they believed to be historical), and the partial example afforded by the Spartan women; who, though no less subordinate by law than in other Greek states, were more free in fact, and being trained to bodily exercises in the same manner with men, gave ample proof that they were not naturally disqualified for them. There can be little doubt that Spartan experience suggested to Plato, among many other of his doctrines, that of the social and political equality of the two sexes.

But, it will be said, the rule of men over women differs from all these others in not being a rule of force : it is accepted voluntarily ; women make no complaint, and are consenting parties to it. In the first place, a great number of women do not accept it. Ever since there have been women able to make their sentiments known by their writings (the only mode of publicity which society permits to them), an increasing number of them have recorded protests against their present social condition : and recently many thousands of them, headed by the most eminent women known to the public, have petitioned Parliament for their admission to the Parliamentary Suffrage. The claim of women to be educated as solidly, and in the same branches of knowledge, as men, is urged with growing intensity, and with a great prospect of success ; while the demand for their admission into professions and occupations hitherto closed against them, becomes every year more urgent. Though there are not in this country, as there are in the United States, periodical Conventions and an organized party to agitate for the Rights of Women, there is a numerous and active Society organized and managed by women, for the more limited object of obtaining the political franchise. Nor is it only in our own country and in America that women are beginning to protest, more or less collectively, against the disabilities under which they labour. France, and Italy, and Switzerland, and Russia now afford examples of the same thing. How many more women there are who silently cherish similar aspirations, no one can possibly know; but there are abundant tokens how many *would* cherish them, were they not so strenuously taught to repress them as contrary to the proprieties of their sex. It must be remembered, also, that no enslaved class ever asked for complete liberty at once. When Simon de Montfort called the deputies of the commons to sit for the first time in Parliament, did any of them dream of demanding that an assembly, elected by their constituents, should make and destroy ministries, and dictate to the king in affairs of state? No such thought entered into the imagination of the most ambitious of them. The nobility had already these pretensions; the commons pretended to nothing but to be exempt from arbitrary taxation, and from the gross individual oppression of the king's officers. It is a political law of nature that those who are under any power of ancient origin, never begin by complaining of the power itself, but only of its oppressive exercise. There is never any want of women who complain of ill usage by their husbands. There would be infinitely more, if complaint were not the greatest of all provocatives to a repetition and increase of the ill usage. It is this which frustrates all attempts to maintain the power but protect the woman against its abuses. In no other case (except that of a child) is the person who has been proved judicially to have suffered an injury, replaced under the physical power of the culprit who inflicted it. Accordingly wives, even in the most extreme and protracted cases of bodily ill usage, hardly ever dare avail themselves of the laws made for their protection : and if, in a moment of irrepressible indignation, or by the interference of neighbours, they are induced to do so, their whole effort afterwards is to disclose as little as they can, and to beg off their tyrant from his merited chastisement.

All causes, social and natural, combine to make it unlikely that women should be collectively rebellious to the power of men. They are so far in a position different from all other subject classes, that their masters require something more from them than actual service. Men do not want solely the obedience of women, they want their sentiments. All men, except the most brutish, desire to have, in the woman most nearly connected with them, not a forced slave but a willing one, not a slave merely, but a favourite.

They have therefore put everything in practice to enslave their minds. The masters of all other slaves rely, for maintaining obedience, on fear; either fear of themselves, or religious fears. The masters of women wanted more than simple obedience, and they turned the whole force of education to effect their purpose. All women are brought up from the very earliest years in the belief that their ideal of character is the very opposite to that of men; not self-will, and government by self-control, but submission, and yielding to the control of others. All the moralities tell them that it is the duty of women, and all the current sentimentalities that it is their nature, to live for others; to make complete abnegation of themselves, and to have no life but in their affections. And by their affections are meant the only ones they are allowed to have—those to the men with whom they are connected, or to the children who constitute an additional and indefeasible tie between them and a man. When we put together three things—first, the natural attraction between opposite sexes; secondly, the wife's entire dependence on the husband, every privilege or pleasure she has being either his gift, or depending entirely on his will; and lastly, that the principal object of human pursuit, consideration, and all objects of social ambition, can in general be sought or obtained by her only through

him, it would be a miracle if the object of being
attractive to men had not become the polar star
of feminine education and formation of character.
And, this great means of influence over the minds
of women having been acquired, an instinct of
selfishness made men avail themselves of it to
the utmost as a means of holding women in
subjection, by representing to them meekness,
submissiveness, and resignation of all individual
will into the hands of a man, as an essential
part of sexual attractiveness. Can it be doubted
that any of the other yokes which mankind have
succeeded in breaking, would have subsisted till
now if the same means had existed, and had been
as sedulously used, to bow down their minds to it ?
If it had been made the object of the life of every
young plebeian to find personal favour in the
eyes of some patrician, of every young serf with
some seigneur ; if domestication with him, and
a share of his personal affections, had been held
out as the prize which they all should look out
for, the most gifted and aspiring being able to
reckon on the most desirable prizes ; and if, when
this prize had been obtained, they had been shut
out by a wall of brass from all interests not
centering in him, all feelings and desires but
those which he shared or inculcated ; would not
serfs and seigneurs, plebeians and patricians, have
been as broadly distinguished at this day as men

and women are? and would not all but a thinker here and there, have believed the distinction to be a fundamental and unalterable fact in human nature?

The preceding considerations are amply sufficient to show that custom, however universal it may be, affords in this case no presumption, and ought not to create any prejudice, in favour of the arrangements which place women in social and political subjection to men. But I may go farther, and maintain that the course of history, and the tendencies of progressive human society, afford not only no presumption in favour of this system of inequality of rights, but a strong one against it; and that, so far as the whole course of human improvement up to this time, the whole stream of modern tendencies, warrants any inference on the subject, it is, that this relic of the past is discordant with the future, and must necessarily disappear.

For, what is the peculiar character of the modern world—the difference which chiefly distinguishes modern institutions, modern social ideas, modern life itself, from those of times long past? It is, that human beings are no longer born to their place in life, and chained down by an inexorable bond to the place they are born to, but are free to employ their faculties, and such favourable chances as offer, to achieve the lot which

may appear to them most desirable. Human
society of old was constituted on a very different
principle. All were born to a fixed social position, and were mostly kept in it by law, or interdicted from any means by which they could
emerge from it. As some men are born white
and others black, so some were born slaves and
others freemen and citizens ; some were born
patricians, others plebeians; some were born feudal
nobles, others commoners and *roturiers*. A slave
or serf could never make himself free, nor,
except by the will of his master, become so.
In most European countries it was not till
towards the close of the middle ages, and as a
consequence of the growth of regal power, that
commoners could be ennobled. Even among nobles,
the eldest son was born the exclusive heir to the
paternal possessions, and a long time elapsed before
it was fully established that the father could dis-
inherit him. Among the industrious classes, only
those who were born members of a guild, or were
admitted into it by its members, could lawfully
practise their calling within its local limits ; and
nobody could practise any calling deemed important, in any but the legal manner—by processes authoritatively prescribed. Manufacturers
have stood in the pillory for presuming to carry
on their business by new and improved methods.
In modern Europe, and most in those parts of

it which have participated most largely in all other modern improvements, diametrically opposite doctrines now prevail. Law and government do not undertake to prescribe by whom any social or industrial operation shall or shall not be conducted, or what modes of conducting them shall be lawful. These things are left to the unfettered choice of individuals. Even the laws which required that workmen should serve an apprenticeship, have in this country been repealed : there being ample assurance that in all cases in which an apprenticeship is necessary, its necessity will suffice to enforce it. The old theory was, that the least possible should be left to the choice of the individual agent; that all he had to do should, as far as practicable, be laid down for him by superior wisdom. Left to himself he was sure to go wrong. The modern conviction, the fruit of a thousand years of experience, is, that things in which the individual is the person directly interested, never go right but as they are left to his own discretion; and that any regulation of them by authority, except to protect the rights of others, is sure to be mischievous. This conclusion, slowly arrived at, and not adopted until almost every possible application of the contrary theory had been made with disastrous result, now (in the industrial department) prevails universally in the most advanced

countries, almost universally in all that have
pretensions to any sort of advancement. It is
not that all processes are supposed to be equally
good, or all persons to be equally qualified for
everything; but that freedom of individual
choice is now known to be the only thing
which procures the adoption of the best processes, and throws each operation into the hands
of those who are best qualified for it. Nobody
thinks it necessary to make a law that only a
strong-armed man shall be a blacksmith. Freedom and competition suffice to make blacksmiths
strong-armed men, because the weak-armed can
earn more by engaging in occupations for which
they are more fit. In consonance with this
doctrine, it is felt to be an overstepping of the
proper bounds of authority to fix beforehand,
on some general presumption, that certain persons are not fit to do certain things. It is now
thoroughly known and admitted that if some
such presumptions exist, no such presumption is
infallible. Even if it be well grounded in a
majority of cases, which it is very likely not
to be, there will be a minority of exceptional
cases in which it does not hold: and in those
it is both an injustice to the individuals, and
a detriment to society, to place barriers in the
way of their using their faculties for their own
benefit and for that of others. In the cases,

on the other hand, in which the unfitness is
real, the ordinary motives of human conduct
will on the whole suffice to prevent the incompetent person from making, or from persisting
in, the attempt.

If this general principle of social and economical science is not true; if individuals, with
such help as they can derive from the opinion
of those who know them, are not better judges
than the law and the government, of their
own capacities and vocation; the world cannot
too soon abandon this principle, and return to
the old system of regulations and disabilities.
But if the principle is true, we ought to act
as if we believed it, and not to ordain that to
be born a girl instead of a boy, any more
than to be born black instead of white, or a
commoner instead of a nobleman, shall decide
the person's position through all life — shall
interdict people from all the more elevated
social positions, and from all, except a few,
respectable occupations. Even were we to admit
the utmost that is ever pretended as to the
superior fitness of men for all the functions now
reserved to them, the same argument applies
which forbids a legal qualification for members of
Parliament. If only once in a dozen years the
conditions of eligibility exclude a fit person,
there is a real loss, while the exclusion of thou-

sands of unfit persons is no gain; for if the constitution of the electoral body disposes them to choose unfit persons, there are always plenty of such persons to choose from. In all things of any difficulty and importance, those who can do them well are fewer than the need, even with the most unrestricted latitude of choice: and any limitation of the field of selection deprives society of some chances of being served by the competent, without ever saving it from the incompetent.

At present, in the more improved countries, the disabilities of women are the only case, save one, in which laws and institutions take persons at their birth, and ordain that they shall never in all their lives be allowed to compete for certain things. The one exception is that of royalty. Persons still are born to the throne; no one, not of the reigning family, can ever occupy it, and no one even of that family can, by any means but the course of hereditary succession, attain it. All other dignities and social advantages are open to the whole male sex: many indeed are only attainable by wealth, but wealth may be striven for by any one, and is actually obtained by many men of the very humblest origin. The difficulties, to the majority, are indeed insuperable without the aid of fortunate accidents; but no male human being is under any legal ban: neither law nor opinion superadd artificial obstacles to the natural ones. Royalty, as I have said, is excepted : but in this case every one feels it to be an exception—an anomaly in the modern world, in marked opposition to its customs and principles, and to be justified only by extraordinary special expediencies, which, though individuals and nations differ in estimating their weight, unquestionably do in fact exist. But in this exceptional case, in which a high social function is, for important reasons, bestowed on birth instead of being put up to competition, all free nations contrive to adhere in substance to the principle from which they nominally derogate ; for they circumscribe this high function by conditions avowedly intended to prevent the person to whom it ostensibly belongs from really performing it ; while the person by whom it is performed, the responsible minister, does obtain the post by a competition from which no full-grown citizen of the male sex is legally excluded. The disabilities, therefore, to which women are subject from the mere fact of their birth, are the solitary examples of the kind in modern legislation. In no instance except this, which comprehends half the human race, are the higher social functions closed against any one by a fatality of birth which no exertions, and no change of circumstances, can overcome ; for even religious disabilities (besides that in England and in Europe they have practically almost ceased to exist) do not close any career to the disqualified person in case of conversion.

The social subordination of women thus stands out an isolated fact in modern social institutions; a solitary breach of what has become their fundamental law; a single relic of an old world of thought and practice exploded in everything else, but retained in the one thing of most universal interest; as if a gigantic dolmen, or a vast temple of Jupiter Olympius, occupied the site of St. Paul's and received daily worship, while the surrounding Christian churches were only resorted to on fasts and festivals. This entire discrepancy between one social fact and all those which accompany it, and the radical opposition between its nature and the progressive movement which is the boast of the modern world, and which has successively swept away everything else of an analogous character, surely affords, to a conscientious observer of human tendencies, serious matter for reflection. It raises a primâ facie presumption on the unfavourable side, far outweighing any which custom and usage could in such circumstances create on the favourable; and should at least suffice to make this, like the choice between republicanism and royalty, a balanced question.

The least that can be demanded is, that the

question should not be considered as prejudged by existing fact and existing opinion, but open to discussion on its merits, as a question of justice and expediency: the decision on this, as on any of the other social arrangements of mankind, depending on what an enlightened estimate of tendencies and consequences may show to be most advantageous to humanity in general, without distinction of sex. And the discussion must be a real discussion, descending to foundations, and not resting satisfied with vague and general assertions. It will not do, for instance, to assert in general terms, that the experience of mankind has pronounced in favour of the existing system. Experience cannot possibly have decided between two courses, so long as there has only been experience of one. If it be said that the doctrine of the equality of the sexes rests only on theory, it must be remembered that the contrary doctrine also has only theory to rest upon. All that is proved in its favour by direct experience, is that mankind have been able to exist under it, and to attain the degree of improvement and prosperity which we now see; but whether that prosperity has been attained sooner, or is now greater, than it would have been under the other system, experience does not say. On the other hand, experience does say, that every step in improvement has been so invariably accompanied by a step made in raising the social position of women, that historians and philosophers have been led to adopt their elevation or debasement as on the whole the surest test and most correct measure of the civilization of a people or an age. Through all the progressive period of human history, the condition of women has been approaching nearer to equality with men. This does not of itself prove that the assimilation must go on to complete equality; but it assuredly affords some presumption that such is the case.

Neither does it avail anything to say that the *nature* of the two sexes adapts them to their present functions and position, and renders these appropriate to them. Standing on the ground of common sense and the constitution of the human mind, I deny that any one knows, or can know, the nature of the two sexes, as long as they have only been seen in their present relation to one another. If men had ever been found in society without women, or women without men, or if there had been a society of men and women in which the women were not under the control of the men, something might have been positively known about the mental and moral differences which may be inherent in the nature of each. What is now called the nature of women is an eminently artificial thing—the result of forced repression in some directions, unnatural stimulation in others. It may be asserted without scruple, that no other class of dependents have had their character so entirely distorted from its natural proportions by their relation with their masters ; for, if conquered and slave races have been, in some respects, more forcibly repressed, whatever in them has not been crushed down by an iron heel has generally been let alone, and if left with any liberty of development, it has developed itself according to its own laws; but in the case of women, a hot-house and stove cultivation has always been carried on of some of the capabilities of their nature, for the benefit and pleasure of their masters. Then, because certain products of the general vital force sprout luxuriantly and reach a great development in this heated atmosphere and under this active nurture and watering, while other shoots from the same root, which are left outside in the wintry air, with ice purposely heaped all round them, have a stunted growth, and some are burnt off with fire and disappear; men, with that inability to recognise their own work which distinguishes the unanalytic mind, indolently believe that the tree grows of itself in the way they have made it grow, and that it would die if one half of it were not kept in a vapour bath and the other half in the snow.

Of all difficulties which impede the progress

of thought, and the formation of well-grounded
opinions on life and social arrangements, the
greatest is now the unspeakable ignorance and
inattention of mankind in respect to the influences which form human character. Whatever
any portion of the human species now are, or
seem to be, such, it is supposed, they have a
natural tendency to be : even when the most
elementary knowledge of the circumstances in
which they have been placed, clearly points out
the causes that made them what they are.
Because a cottier deeply in arrears to his land-
lord is not industrious, there are people who
think that the Irish are naturally idle. Because
constitutions can be overthrown when the authorities appointed to execute them turn their arms
against them, there are people who think the
French incapable of free government. Because
the Greeks cheated the Turks, and the Turks only
plundered the Greeks, there are persons who
think that the Turks are naturally more sincere :
and because women, as is often said, care nothing
about politics except their personalities, it is
supposed that the general good is naturally less
interesting to women than to men. History,
which is now so much better understood than
formerly, teaches another lesson : if only by showing the extraordinary susceptibility of human
nature to external influences, and the extreme

variableness of those of its manifestations which are supposed to be most universal and uniform. But in history, as in travelling, men usually see only what they already had in their own minds ; and few learn much from history, who do not bring much with them to its study.

Hence, in regard to that most difficult question, what are the natural differences between the two sexes—a subject on which it is impossible in the present state of society to obtain complete and correct knowledge—while almost everybody dogmatizes upon it, almost all neglect and make light of the only means by which any partial insight can be obtained into it. This is, an analytic study of the most important department of psychology, the laws of the influence of circumstances on character. For, however great and apparently ineradicable the moral and intellectual differences between men and women might be, the evidence of their being natural differences could only be negative. Those only could be inferred to be natural which could not possibly be artificial—the residuum, after deducting every characteristic of either sex which can admit of being explained from education or external circumstances. The profoundest knowledge of the laws of the formation of character is indispensable to entitle any one to affirm even that there is any difference, much more what the difference is, between the two sexes considered as moral and rational beings; and since no one, as yet, has that knowledge, (for there is hardly any subject which, in proportion to its importance, has been so little studied), no one is thus far entitled to any positive opinion on the subject. Conjectures are all that can at present be made; conjectures more or less probable, according as more or less authorized by such knowledge as we yet have of the laws of psychology, as applied to the formation of character.

Even the preliminary knowledge, what the differences between the sexes now are, apart from all question as to how they are made what they are, is still in the crudest and most incomplete state. Medical practitioners and physiologists have ascertained, to some extent, the differences in bodily constitution; and this is an important element to the psychologist: but hardly any medical practitioner is a psychologist. Respecting the mental characteristics of women; their observations are of no more worth than those of common men. It is a subject on which nothing final can be known, so long as those who alone can really know it, women themselves, have given but little testimony, and that little, mostly suborned. It is easy to know stupid women. Stupidity is much the same all the world over. A stupid person's notions and feelings may confidently be inferred from those which prevail in the circle by which the person is surrounded. Not so with those whose opinions and feelings are an emanation from their own nature and faculties. It is only a man here and there who has any tolerable knowledge of the character even of the women of his own family. I do not mean, of their capabilities; these nobody knows, not even themselves, because most of them have never been called out. I mean their actually existing thoughts and feelings. Many a man thinks he perfectly understands women, because he has had amatory relations with several, perhaps with many of them. If he is a good observer, and his experience extends to quality as well as quantity, he may have learnt something of one narrow department of their nature—an important department, no doubt. But of all the rest of it, few persons are generally more ignorant, because there are few from whom it is so carefully hidden. The most favourable case which a man can generally have for studying the character of a woman, is that of his own wife: for the opportunities are greater, and the cases of complete sympathy not so unspeakably rare. And in fact, this is the source from which any knowledge worth having on the subject has, I believe, generally come. But most men have not had the opportunity of studying in this way more than a single case : accordingly one can, to an almost laughable degree, infer what a man's wife is like, from his opinions about women in general. To make even this one case yield any result, the woman must be worth knowing, and the man not only a competent judge, but of a character so sympathetic in itself, and so well adapted to hers, that he can either read her mind by sympathetic intuition, or has nothing in himself which makes her shy of disclosing it. Hardly anything, I believe, can be more rare than this conjunction. It often happens that there is the most complete unity of feeling and community of interests as to all external things, yet the one has as little admission into the internal life of the other as if they were common acquaintance. Even with true affection, authority on the one side and subordination on the other prevent perfect confidence. Though nothing may be intentionally withheld, much is not shown. In the analogous relation of parent and child, the corresponding phenomenon must have been in the observation of every one. As between father and son, how many are the cases in which the father, in spite of real affection on both sides, obviously to all the world does not know, nor suspect, parts of the son's character familiar to his companions and equals. The truth is, that the position of looking up to another is extremely unpropitious to complete sincerity and openness with him. The fear of losing ground in his opinion or in his feelings is so strong, that even in an upright character, there is an unconscious tendency to show only the best side, or the side which, though not the best, is that which he most likes to see : and it may be confidently said that thorough knowledge of one another hardly ever exists, but between persons who, besides being intimates, are equals. How much more true, then, must all this be, when the one is not only under the authority of the other, but has it inculcated on her as a duty to reckon everything else subordinate to his comfort and pleasure, and to let him neither see nor feel anything coming from her, except what is agreeable to him. All these difficulties stand in the way of a man's obtaining any thorough knowledge even of the one woman whom alone, in general, he has sufficient opportunity of studying. When we further consider that to understand one woman is not necessarily to understand any other woman ; that even if he could study many women of one rank, or of one country, he would not thereby understand women of other ranks or countries ; and even if he did, they are still only the women of a single period of history ; we may safely assert that the knowledge which men can acquire of women, even as they have

been and are, without reference to what they
might be, is wretchedly imperfect and superficial,
and always will be so, until women themselves
have told all that they have to tell.

And this time has not come; nor will it come
otherwise than gradually. It is but of yesterday
that women have either been qualified by literary
accomplishments, or permitted by society, to tell
anything to the general public. As yet very
few of them dare tell anything, which men, on
whom their literary success depends, are unwilling to hear. Let us remember in what manner,
up to a very recent time, the expression, even
by a male author, of uncustomary opinions, or
what are deemed eccentric feelings, usually was,
and in some degree still is, received; and we may
form some faint conception under what impedi-
ments a woman, who is brought up to think
custom and opinion her sovereign rule, attempts
to express in books anything drawn from the
depths of her own nature. The greatest woman
who has left writings behind her sufficient to
give her an eminent rank in the literature of her
country, thought it necessary to prefix as a motto
to her boldest work, " Un homme peut braver
l'opinion; une femme doit s'y soumettre."* The
greater part of what women write about women
is mere sycophancy to men. In the case of un-

* Title-page of Mme. de Stael's " Delphine."

married women, much of it seems only intended
to increase their chance of a husband. Many,
both married and unmarried, overstep the mark,
and inculcate a servility beyond what is desired
or relished by any man, except the very vulgarest.
But this is not so often the case as, even at a
quite late period, it still was. Literary women
are becoming more freespoken, and more willing
to express their real sentiments. Unfortunately,
in this country especially, they are themselves
such artificial products, that their sentiments are
compounded of a small element of individual
observation and consciousness, and a very large
one of acquired associations. This will be less
and less the case, but it will remain true to a
great extent, as long as social institutions do not
admit the same free development of originality
in women which is possible to men. When that
time comes, and not before, we shall see, and
not merely hear, as much as it is necessary to
know of the nature of women, and the adaptation
of other things to it.

I have dwelt so much on the difficulties which
at present obstruct any real knowledge by men
of the true nature of women, because in this as
in so many other things "opinio copiæ inter
maximas causas inopiæ est;" and there is little
chance of reasonable thinking on the matter,
while people flatter themselves that they perfectly

understand a subject of which most men know absolutely nothing, and of which it is at present impossible that any man, or all men taken together, should have knowledge which can qualify them to lay down the law to women as to what is, or is not, their vocation. Happily, no such knowledge is necessary for any practical purpose connected with the position of women in relation to society and life. For, according to all the principles involved in modern society, the question rests with women themselves—to be decided by their own experience, and by the use of their own faculties. There are no means of finding what either one person or many can do, but by trying—and no means by which any one else can discover for them what it is for their happiness to do or leave undone.

One thing we may be certain of—that what is contrary to women's nature to do, they never will be made to do by simply giving their nature free play. The anxiety of mankind to interfere in behalf of nature, for fear lest nature should not succeed in effecting its purpose, is an altogether unnecessary solicitude. What women by nature cannot do, it is quite superfluous to forbid them from doing. What they can do, but not so well as the men who are their competitors, competition suffices to exclude them from; since nobody asks for protective duties and bounties in favour of women; it is only asked that the present bounties and protective duties in favour of men should be recalled. If women have a greater natural inclination for some things than for others, there is no need of laws or social inculcation to make the majority of them do the former in preference to the latter. Whatever women's services are most wanted for, the free play of competition will hold out the strongest inducements to them to undertake. And, as the words imply, they are most wanted for the things for which they are most fit; by the apportionment of which to them, the collective faculties of the two sexes can be applied on the whole with the greatest sum of valuable result.

The general opinion of men is supposed to be, that the natural vocation of a woman is that of a wife and mother. I say, is supposed to be, because, judging from acts—from the whole of the present constitution of society—one might infer that their opinion was the direct contrary. They might be supposed to think that the alleged natural vocation of women was of all things the most repugnant to their nature; insomuch that if they are free to do anything else—if any other means of living, or occupation of their time and faculties, is open, which has any chance of appearing desirable to them—there

will not be enough of them who will be willing
to accept the condition said to be natural to
them. If this is the real opinion of men in
general, it would be well that it should be
spoken out. I should like to hear somebody
openly enunciating the doctrine (it is already
implied in much that is written on the subject)—" It is necessary to society that women
should marry and produce children. They will
not do so unless they are compelled. Therefore
it is necessary to compel them." The merits of
the case would then be clearly defined. It
would be exactly that of the slaveholders of
South Carolina and Louisiana. " It is necessary
that cotton and sugar should be grown. White
men cannot produce them. Negroes will not,
for any wages which we choose to give. *Ergo*
they must be compelled." An illustration still
closer to the point is that of impressment.
Sailors must absolutely be had to defend the
country. It often happens that they will not
voluntarily enlist. Therefore there must be
the power of forcing them. How often has
this logic been used! and, but for one flaw
in it, without doubt it would have been successful up to this day. But it is open to the
retort—First pay the sailors the honest value
of their labour. When you have made it as
well worth their while to serve you, as to work for

other employers, you will have no more difficulty
than others have in obtaining their services.
To this there is no logical answer except " I will
not :" and as people are now not only ashamed,
but are not desirous, to rob the labourer of his
hire, impressment is no longer advocated. Those
who attempt to force women into marriage by
closing all other doors against them, lay themselves open to a similar retort. If they mean
what they say, their opinion must evidently be,
that men do not render the married condition
so desirable to women, as to induce them to
accept it for its own recommendations. It is
not a sign of one's thinking the boon one offers
very attractive, when one allows only Hobson's
choice, " that or none." And here, I believe,
is the clue to the feelings of those men, who
have a real antipathy to the equal freedom of
women.   I believe they are afraid, not lest
women should be unwilling to marry, for I
do not think that any one in reality has that
apprehension; but lest they should insist that
marriage should be on equal conditions ; lest
all women of spirit and capacity should prefer
doing almost anything else, not in their own
eyes degrading, rather than marry, when marrying is giving themselves a master, and a master
too of all their earthly possessions. And truly,
if this consequence were necessarily incident to

marriage, I think that the apprehension would be very well founded. I agree in thinking it probable that few women, capable of anything else, would, unless under an irresistible *entrainement*, rendering them for the time insensible to anything but itself, choose such a lot, when any other means were open to them of filling a conventionally honourable place in life: and if men are determined that the law of marriage shall be a law of despotism, they are quite right, in point of mere policy, in leaving to women only Hobson's choice. But, in that case, all that has been done in the modern world to relax the chain on the minds of women, has been a mistake. They never should have been allowed to receive a literary education. Women who read, much more women who write, are, in the existing constitution of things, a contradiction and a disturbing element: and it was wrong to bring women up with any acquirements but those of an odalisque, or of a domestic servant.

CHAPTER II.

IT will be well to commence the detailed discussion of the subject by the particular
branch of it to which the course of our observations has led us: the conditions which the laws
of this and all other countries annex to the
marriage contract. Marriage being the destina-
tion appointed by society for women, the prospect
they are brought up to, and the object which it
is intended should be sought by all of them, except those who are too little attractive to be
chosen by any man as his companion; one might
have supposed that everything would have been
done to make this condition as eligible to them
as possible, that they might have no cause to
regret being denied the option of any other.
Society, however, both in this, and, at first, in all
other cases, has preferred to attain its object by
foul rather than fair means: but this is the only
case in which it has substantially persisted in
them even to the present day. Originally women
were taken by force, or regularly sold by their
father to the husband. Until a late period in

European history, the father had the power to dispose of his daughter in marriage at his own will and pleasure, without any regard to hers. The Church, indeed, was so far faithful to a better morality as to require a formal " yes" from the woman at the marriage ceremony; but there was nothing to shew that the consent was other than compulsory; and it was practically impossible for the girl to refuse compliance if the father persevered, except perhaps when she might obtain the protection of religion by a determined resolution to take monastic vows. After marriage, the man had anciently (but this was anterior to Christianity) the power of life and death over his wife. She could invoke no law against him; he was her sole tribunal and law. For a long time he could repudiate her, but she had no corresponding power in regard to him. By the old laws of England, the husband was called the *lord* of the wife; he was literally regarded as her sovereign, inasmuch that the murder of a man by his wife was called treason (*petty* as distinguished from *high* treason), and was more cruelly avenged than was usually the case with high treason, for the penalty was burning to death. Because these various enormities have fallen into disuse (for most of them were never formally abolished, or not until they had long ceased to be practised) men suppose that all is now as it should be in regard to the marriage contract; and we are continually told that civilization and Christianity have restored to the woman her just rights. Meanwhile the wife is the actual bond--servant of her husband : no less so, as far as legal obligation goes, than slaves commonly so called. She vows a lifelong obedience to him at the altar, and is held to it all through her life by law. Casuists may say that the obligation of obedience stops short of participation in crime, but it certainly extends to everything else. She can do no act whatever but by his permission, at least tacit. She can acquire no property but for him ; the instant it becomes hers, even if by inheritance, it becomes *ipso facto* his. In this respect the wife's position under the common law of England is worse than that of slaves in the laws of many countries : by the Roman law, for example, a slave might have his peculium, which to a certain extent the law guaranteed to him for his exclusive use. The higher classes in this country have given an analogous advantage to their women, through special contracts setting aside the law, by conditions of pin-money, &c.: since parental feeling being stronger with fathers than the class feeling of their own sex, a father generally prefers his own daughter to a son-in-law who is a stranger to him. By means of settlements, the rich usually contrive to withdraw the whole or part of the inherited property of the wife from the absolute control of the husband: but they do not succeed in keeping it under her own control; the utmost they can do only prevents the husband from squandering it, at the same time debarring the rightful owner from its use. The property itself is out of the reach of both; and as to the income derived from it, the form of settlement most favourable to the wife (that called " to her separate use") only precludes the husband from receiving it instead of her: it must pass through her hands, but if he takes it from her by personal violence as soon as she receives it, he can neither be punished, nor compelled to restitution. This is the amount of the protection which, under the laws of this country, the most powerful nobleman can give to his own daughter as respects her husband. In the immense majority of cases there is no settlement: and the absorption of all rights, all property, as well as all freedom of action, is complete. The two are called " one person in law," for the purpose of inferring that whatever is hers is his, but the parallel inference is never drawn that whatever is his is hers; the maxim is not applied against the man, except to make him responsible to third parties for her acts, as a master is for the acts of his slaves or of his cattle. I am far from pretending that wives are in general no better treated than slaves; but no slave is a slave to the same lengths, and in so full a sense of the word, as a wife is. Hardly any slave, except one immediately attached to the master's person, is a slave at all hours and all minutes; in general he has, like a soldier, his fixed task, and when it is done, or when he is off duty, he disposes, within certain limits, of his own time, and has a family life into which the master rarely intrudes. " Uncle Tom" under his first master had his own life in his " cabin," almost as much as any man whose work takes him away from home, is able to have in his own family. But it cannot be so with the wife. Above all, a female slave has (in Christian countries) an admitted right, and is considered under a moral obligation, to refuse to her master the last familiarity. Not so the wife : however brutal a tyrant she may unfortunately be chained to—though she may know that he hates her, though it may be his daily pleasure to torture her, and though she may feel it impossible not to loathe him—he can claim from her and enforce the lowest degradation of a human being, that of being made the instrument of an animal function contrary to her inclinations. While she is held in this worst description of slavery as to her own person, what is her position in regard to the children in whom she and her master have a joint interest?

They are by law *his* children.   He alone has any legal rights over them.   Not one act can she do towards or in relation to them, except by delegation from him.   Even after he is dead she is not their legal guardian, unless he by will has made her so.   He could even send them away from her, and deprive her of the means of seeing or corresponding with them, until this power was in some degree restricted by Serjeant Talfourd's Act.   This is her legal state.   And from this state she has no means of withdrawing herself.   If she leaves her husband, she can take nothing with her, neither her children nor anything which is rightfully her own.   If he chooses, he can compel her to return, by law, or by physical force; or he may content himself with seizing for his own use anything which she may earn, or which may be given to her by her relations.   It is only legal separation by a decree of a court of justice, which entitles her to live apart, without being forced back into the custody of an exasperated jailer—or which empowers her to apply any earnings to her own use, without fear that a man whom perhaps she has not seen for twenty years will pounce upon her some day and carry all off.   This legal separation, until lately, the courts of justice would only give at an expense which made it inaccessible to any one out of the higher ranks.   Even now it is only given in cases of desertion, or of the extreme of cruelty; and yet complaints are made every day that it is granted too easily. Surely, if a woman is denied any lot in life but that of being the personal body-servant of a despot, and is dependent for everything upon the chance of finding one who may be disposed to make a favourite of her instead of merely a drudge, it is a very cruel aggravation of her fate that she should be allowed to try this chance only once. The natural sequel and corollary from this state of things would be, that since her all in life depends upon obtaining a good master, she should be allowed to change again and again until she finds one. I am not saying that she ought to be allowed this privilege. That is a totally different consideration. The question of divorce, in the sense involving liberty of remarriage, is one into which it is foreign to my purpose to enter. All I now say is, that to those to whom nothing but servitude is allowed, the free choice of servitude is the only, though a most insufficient, alleviation. Its refusal completes the assimilation of the wife to the slave—and the slave under not the mildest form of slavery: for in some slave codes the slave could, under certain circumstances of ill usage, legally compel the master to sell him. But no amount of ill usage, without adultery superadded, will in England free a wife from her tormentor.

I have no desire to exaggerate, nor does the case stand in any need of exaggeration. I have described the wife's legal position, not her actual treatment. The laws of most countries are far worse than the people who execute them, and many of them are only able to remain laws by being seldom or never carried into effect. If married life were all that it might be expected to be, looking to the laws alone, society would be a hell upon earth. Happily there are both feelings and interests which in many men exclude, and in most, greatly temper, the impulses and propensities which lead to tyranny: and of those feelings, the tie which connects a man with his wife affords, in a normal state of things, incomparably the strongest example. The only tie which at all approaches to it, that between him and his children, tends, in all save exceptional cases, to strengthen, instead of conflicting with, the first. Because this is true; because men in general do not inflict, nor women suffer, all the misery which could be inflicted and suffered if the full power of tyranny with which the man is legally invested were acted on; the defenders of the existing form of the institution think that all its iniquity is justified, and that any complaint is merely quarrelling with the evil which is the price paid for every great good. But the mitigations in practice, which are compatible with maintaining in full legal force this or any other kind of tyranny, instead of being any apology for despotism, only serve to prove what power human nature possesses of reacting against the vilest institutions, and with what vitality the seeds of good as well as those of evil in human character diffuse and propagate themselves. Not a word can be said for despotism in the family which cannot be said for political despotism. Every absolute king does not sit at his window to enjoy the groans of his tortured subjects, nor strips them of their last rag and turns them out to shiver in the road. The despotism of Louis XVI. was not the despotism of Philippe le Bel, or of Nadir Shah, or of Caligula; but it was bad enough to justify the French Revolution, and to palliate even its horrors. If an appeal be made to the intense attachments which exist between wives and their husbands, exactly as much may be said of domestic slavery. It was quite an ordinary fact in Greece and Rome for slaves to submit to death by torture rather than betray their masters. In the proscriptions of the Roman civil wars it was remarked that wives and slaves were heroically faithful, sons very commonly treacherous. Yet we know how cruelly many Romans treated their slaves. But in truth these intense in-

dividual feelings nowhere rise to such a luxuriant
height as under the most atrocious institutions.
It is part of the irony of life, that the strongest
feelings of devoted gratitude of which human
nature seems to be susceptible, are called forth
in human beings towards those who, having the
power entirely to crush their earthly existence,
voluntarily refrain from using that power. How
great a place in most men this sentiment fills, even
in religious devotion, it would be cruel to inquire.
We daily see how much their gratitude to
Heaven appears to be stimulated by the con-
templation of fellow-creatures to whom God
has not been so merciful as he has to themselves.

Whether the institution to be defended is
slavery, political absolutism, or the absolutism of
the head of a family, we are always expected to
judge of it from its best instances; and we are
presented with pictures of loving exercise of
authority on one side, loving submission to it on
the other—superior wisdom ordering all things
for the greatest good of the dependents, and surrounded by their smiles and benedictions. All
this would be very much to the purpose if any
one pretended that there are no such things as
good men. Who doubts that there may be great
goodness, and great happiness, and great affection,
under the absolute government of a good man?
Meanwhile, laws and institutions require to be

adapted, not to good men, but to bad. Marriage is not an institution designed for a select few. Men are not required, as a preliminary to the marriage ceremony, to prove by testimonials that they are fit to be trusted with the exercise of absolute power. The tie of affection and obligation to a wife and children is very strong with those whose general social feelings are strong, and with many who are little sensible to any other social ties; but there are all degrees of sensibility and insensibility to it, as there are all grades of goodness and wickedness in men, down to those whom no ties will bind, and on whom society has no action but through its *ultima ratio,* the penalties of the law. In every grade of this descending scale are men to whom are committed all the legal powers of a husband. The vilest malefactor has some wretched woman tied to him, against whom he can commit any atrocity except killing her, and, if tolerably cautious, can do that without much danger of the legal penalty. And how many thousands are there among the lowest classes in every country, who, without being in a legal sense malefactors in any other respect, because in every other quarter their aggressions meet with resistance, indulge the utmost habitual excesses of bodily violence towards the unhappy wife, who alone, at least of grown persons, can neither repel nor escape from their brutality; and towards whom the excess of dependence inspires their mean and savage natures, not with a generous forbearance, and a point of honour to behave well to one whose lot in life is trusted entirely to their kindness, but on the contrary with a notion that the law has delivered her to them as their thing, to be used at their pleasure, and that they are not expected to practise the consideration towards her which is required from them towards everybody else. The law, which till lately left even these atrocious extremes of domestic oppression practically unpunished, has within these few years made some feeble attempts to repress them. But its attempts have done little, and cannot be expected to do much, because it is contrary to reason and experience to suppose that there can be any real check to brutality, consistent with leaving the victim still in the power of the executioner. Until a conviction for personal violence, or at all events a repetition of it after a first conviction, entitles the woman *ipso facto* to a divorce, or at least to a judicial separation, the attempt to repress these "aggravated assaults" by legal penalties will break down for want of a prosecutor, or for want of a witness.

When we consider how vast is the number of men, in any great country, who are little higher than brutes, and that this never prevents them from being able, through the law of marriage, to obtain a victim, the breadth and depth of human misery caused in this shape alone by the abuse of the institution swells to something appalling. Yet these are only the extreme cases. They are the lowest abysses, but there is a sad succession of depth after depth before reaching them. In domestic as in political tyranny, the case of absolute monsters chiefly illustrates the institution by showing that there is scarcely any horror which may not occur under it if the despot pleases, and thus setting in a strong light what must be the terrible frequency of things only a little less atrocious. Absolute fiends are as rare as angels, perhaps rarer: ferocious savages, with occasional touches of humanity, are however very frequent: and in the wide interval which separates these from any worthy representatives of the human species, how many are the forms and gradations of animalism and selfishness, often under an outward varnish of civilization and even cultivation, living at peace with the law, maintaining a creditable appearance to all who are not under their power, yet sufficient often to make the lives of all who are so, a torment and a burthen to them! It would be tiresome to repeat the commonplaces about the unfitness of men in general for power, which, after the political discussions of centuries, every

one knows by heart, were it not that hardly any
one thinks of applying these maxims to the case
in which above all others they are applicable,
that of power, not placed in the hands of a man
here and there, but offered to every adult male,
down to the basest and most ferocious. It is
not because a man is not known to have broken
any of the Ten Commandments, or because he
maintains a respectable character in his dealings
with those whom he cannot compel to have
intercourse with him, or because he does not fly
out into violent bursts of ill-temper against those
who are not obliged to bear with him, that it is
possible to surmise of what sort his conduct will
be in the unrestraint of home. Even the commonest men reserve the violent, the sulky, the
undisguisedly selfish side of their character for
those who have no power to withstand it. The
relation of superiors to dependents is the nursery
of these vices of character, which, wherever else
they exist, are an overflowing from that source.
A man who is morose or violent to his equals,
is sure to be one who has lived among inferiors,
whom he could frighten or worry into submission. If the family in its best forms is, as it is
often said to be, a school of sympathy, tenderness,
and loving forgetfulness of self, it is still oftener,
as respects its chief, a school of wilfulness, overbearingness, unbounded self-indulgence, and a

double-dyed and idealized selfishness, of which
sacrifice itself is only a particular form : the care
for the wife and children being only care for
them as parts of the man's own interests and
belongings, and their individual happiness being
immolated in every shape to his smallest preferences. What better is to be looked for under
the existing form of the institution? We know
that the bad propensities of human nature are
only kept within bounds when they are allowed
no scope for their indulgence. We know that
from impulse and habit, when not from delibe-
rate purpose, almost every one to whom others
yield, goes on encroaching upon them, until a
point is reached at which they are compelled to
resist. Such being the common tendency of
human nature; the almost unlimited power which
present social institutions give to the man over
at least one human being—the one with whom
he resides, and whom he has always present—
this power seeks out and evokes the latent germs
of selfishness in the remotest corners of his
nature—fans its faintest sparks and smouldering
embers—offers to him a license for the indulgence
of those points of his original character which
in all other relations he would have found it necessary to repress and conceal, and the repression
of which would in time have become a second
nature. I know that there is another side to

the question. I grant that the wife, if she cannot effectually resist, can at least retaliate; she, too, can make the man's life extremely uncomfortable, and by that power is able to carry many points which she ought, and many which she ought not, to prevail in. But this instrument of self-protection—which may be called the power of the scold, or the shrewish sanction —has the fatal defect, that it avails most against the least tyrannical superiors, and in favour of the least deserving dependents. It is the weapon of irritable and self-willed women; of those who would make the worst use of power if they themselves had it, and who generally turn this power to a bad use. The amiable cannot use such an instrument, the highminded disdain it. And on the other hand, the husbands against whom it is used most effectively are the gentler and more inoffensive; those who cannot be induced, even by provocation, to resort to any very harsh exercise of authority. The wife's power of being disagreeable generally only establishes a counter-tyranny, and makes victims in their turn chiefly of those husbands who are least inclined to be tyrants.

What is it, then, which really tempers the corrupting effects of the power, and makes it compatible with such amount of good as we actually see? Mere feminine blandishments,

though of great effect in individual instances,
have very little effect in modifying the general
tendencies of the situation ; for their power only
lasts while the woman is young and attractive,
often only while her charm is new, and not
dimmed by familiarity ; and on many men they
have not much influence at any time. The real
mitigating causes are, the personal affection
which is the growth of time, in so far as the man's
nature is susceptible of it, and the woman's
character sufficiently congenial with his to excite
it ; their common interests as regards the children, and their general community of interest
as concerns third persons (to which however there
are very great limitations) ; the real importance
of the wife to his daily comforts and enjoyments,
and the value he consequently attaches to her
on his personal account, which, in a man capable
of feeling for others, lays the foundation of caring
for her on her own ; and lastly, the influence naturally acquired over almost all human beings by
those near to their persons (if not actually disagreeable to them): who, both by their direct entreaties,
and by the insensible contagion of their feelings
and dispositions, are often able, unless counter-
acted by some equally strong personal influence,
to obtain a degree of command over the conduct
of the superior, altogether excessive and un-
reasonable. Through these various means, the

wife frequently exercises even too much power over the man; she is able to affect his conduct in things in which she may not be qualified to influence it for good—in which her influence may be not only unenlightened, but employed on the morally wrong side; and in which he would act better if left to his own prompting. But neither in the affairs of families nor in those of states is power a compensation for the loss of freedom. Her power often gives her what she has no right to, but does not enable her to assert her own rights. A Sultan's favourite slave has slaves under her, over whom she tyrannizes; but the desirable thing would be that she should neither have slaves nor be a slave. By entirely sinking her own existence in her husband; by having no will (or persuading him that she has no will) but his, in anything which regards their joint relation, and by making it the business of her life to work upon his sentiments, a wife may gratify herself by influencing, and very probably perverting, his conduct, in those of his external relations which she has never qualified herself to judge of, or in which she is herself wholly influenced by some personal or other partiality or prejudice. Accordingly, as things now are, those who act most kindly to their wives, are quite as often made worse, as better, by the wife's influence, in respect to all interests extending beyond the family. She is taught that she has no business with things out of that sphere ; and accordingly she seldom has any honest and conscientious opinion on them ; and therefore hardly ever meddles with them for any legitimate purpose, but generally for an interested one. She neither knows nor cares which is the right side in politics, but she knows what will bring in money or invitations, give her husband a title, her son a place, or her daughter a good marriage.

But how, it will be asked, can any society exist without government? In a family, as in a state, some one person must be the ultimate ruler. Who shall decide when married people differ in opinion? Both cannot have their way, yet a decision one way or the other must be come to.

It is not true that in all voluntary association between two people, one of them must be absolute master : still less that the law must determine which of them it shall be. The most frequent case of voluntary association, next to marriage, is partnership in business : and it is not found or thought necessary to enact that in every partnership, one partner shall have entire control over the concern, and the others shall be bound to obey his orders. No one would enter into partnership on terms which would subject him to the responsibilities of a principal, with only the

powers and privileges of a clerk or agent. If
the law dealt with other contracts as it does with
marriage, it would ordain that one partner should
administer the common business as if it was his
private concern; that the others should have only
delegated powers; and that this one should be
designated by some general presumption of law,
for example as being the eldest. The law never
does this: nor does experience show it to be
necessary that any theoretical inequality of power
should exist between the partners, or that the
partnership should have any other conditions than
what they may themselves appoint by their articles
of agreement. Yet it might seem that the exclusive power might be conceded with less danger
to the rights and interests of the inferior, in the
case of partnership than in that of marriage,
since he is free to cancel the power by withdrawing from the connexion. The wife has no
such power, and even if she had, it is almost
always desirable that she should try all measures
before resorting to it.

It is quite true that things which have to
be decided every day, and cannot adjust themselves gradually, or wait for a compromise, ought
to depend on one will: one person must have
their sole control. But it does not follow that
this should always be the same person. The
natural arrangement is a division of powers

between the two; each being absolute in the executive branch of their own department, and any change of system and principle requiring the consent of both. The division neither can nor should be pre-established by the law, since it must depend on individual capacities and suitabilities. If the two persons chose, they might pre-appoint it by the marriage contract, as pecuniary arrangements are now often pre-appointed. There would seldom be any difficulty in deciding such things by mutual consent, unless the marriage was one of those unhappy ones in which all other things, as well as this, become subjects of bickering and dispute. The division of rights would naturally follow the division of duties and functions; and that is already made by consent, or at all events not by law, but by general custom, modified and modifiable at the pleasure of the persons concerned.

The real practical decision of affairs, to whichever may be given the legal authority, will greatly depend, as it even now does, upon comparative qualifications. The mere fact that he is usually the eldest, will in most cases give the preponderance to the man; at least until they both attain a time of life at which the difference in their years is of no importance. There will naturally also be a more potential voice on the side, whichever it is, that brings the means of support. Inequality from this source does not depend on the law of marriage, but on the general conditions of human society, as now constituted. The influence of mental superiority, either general or special, and of superior decision of character, will necessarily tell for much. It always does so at present. And this fact shows how little foundation there is for the apprehension that the powers and responsibilities of partners in life (as of partners in business), cannot be satisfactorily apportioned by agreement between themselves. They always are so apportioned, except in cases in which the marriage institution is a failure. Things never come to an issue of downright power on one side, and obedience on the other, except where the connexion altogether has been a mistake, and it would be a blessing to both parties to be relieved from it. Some may say that the very thing by which an amicable settlement of differences becomes possible, is the power of legal compulsion known to be in reserve; as people submit to an arbitration because there is a court of law in the background, which they know that they can be forced to obey. But to make the cases parallel, we must suppose that the rule of the court of law was, not to try the cause, but to give judgment always for the same side, suppose the defendant. If so, the amenability to it would be a motive with the plaintiff to agree to almost any arbitration, but it would be just the reverse with the defendant. The despotic power which the law gives to the husband may be a reason to make the wife assent to any compromise by which power is practically shared between the two, but it cannot be the reason why the husband does. That there is always among decently conducted people a practical compromise, though one of them at least is under no physical or moral necessity of making it, shows that the natural motives which lead to a voluntary adjustment of the united life of two persons in a manner acceptable to both, do on the whole, except in unfavourable cases, prevail. The matter is certainly not improved by laying down as an ordinance of law, that the superstructure of free government shall be raised upon a legal basis of despotism on one side and subjection on the other, and that every concession which the despot makes may, at his mere pleasure, and without any warning, be recalled. Besides that no freedom is worth much when held on so precarious a tenure, its conditions are not likely to be the most equitable when the law throws so prodigious a weight into one scale; when the adjustment rests between two persons one of whom is declared to be entitled to everything, the other not only entitled to nothing except during the good pleasure of the first, but under the strongest moral and religious obligation not to rebel under any excess of oppression.

A pertinacious adversary, pushed to extremities, may say, that husbands indeed are willing to be reasonable, and to make fair concessions to their partners without being compelled to it, but that wives are not: that if allowed any rights of their own, they will acknowledge no rights at all in any one else, and never will yield in anything, unless they can be compelled, by the man's mere authority, to yield in everything. This would have been said by many persons some generations ago, when satires on women were in vogue, and men thought it a clever thing to insult women for being what men made them. But it will be said by no one now who is worth replying to. It is not the doctrine of the present day that women are less susceptible of good feeling, and consideration for those with whom they are united by the strongest ties, than men are. On the contrary, we are perpetually told that women are better than men, by those who are totally opposed to treating them as if they were as good; so that the saying has passed into a piece of tiresome cant, intended to put a complimentary face upon an injury, and resembling those celebrations of royal clemency which, according to Gulliver, the king of Lilliput always prefixed to his most sanguinary decrees. If women are better than men in anything, it surely is in individual self-sacrifice for those of their own family. But I lay little stress on this, so long as they are universally taught that they are born and created for self-sacrifice. I believe that equality of rights would abate the exaggerated self-abnegation which is the present artificial ideal of feminine character, and that a good woman would not be more self-sacrificing than the best man : but on the other hand, men would be much more unselfish and self-sacrificing than at present, because they would no longer be taught to worship their own will as such a grand thing that it is actually the law for another rational being. There is nothing which men so easily learn as this self-worship : all privileged persons, and all privileged classes, have had it. The more we descend in the scale of humanity, the intenser it is; and most of all in those who are not, and can never expect to be, raised above any one except an unfortunate wife and children. The honourable exceptions are proportionally fewer than in the case of almost any other human infirmity. Philosophy and religion, instead of keeping it in check, are generally suborned to defend it; and nothing controls it but that practical feeling of the equality of human beings, which is the theory of Christianity, but which Christianity will never practically teach, while it sanctions institutions grounded on an arbitrary preference of one human being over another.

There are, no doubt, women, as there are men, whom equality of consideration will not satisfy; with whom there is no peace while any will or wish is regarded but their own. Such persons are a proper subject for the law of divorce. They are only fit to live alone, and no human beings ought to be compelled to associate their lives with them. But the legal subordination tends to make such characters among women more, rather than less, frequent. If the man exerts his whole power, the woman is of course crushed: but if she is treated with indulgence, and permitted to assume power, there is no rule to set limits to her encroachments. The law, not determining her rights, but theoretically allowing her none at all, practically declares that the measure of what she has a right to, is what she can contrive to get.

The equality of married persons before the law, is not only the sole mode in which that particular relation can be made consistent with justice to both sides, and conducive to the happiness of both, but it is the only means of rendering the daily life of mankind, in any

high sense, a school of moral cultivation. Though
the truth may not be felt or generally acknowledged for generations to come, the only school
of genuine moral sentiment is society between
equals. The moral education of mankind has
hitherto emanated chiefly from the law of force,
and is adapted almost solely to the relations
which force creates. In the less advanced
states of society, people hardly recognise any
relation with their equals. To be an equal is
to be an enemy. Society, from its highest place
to its lowest, is one long chain, or rather ladder,
where every individual is either above or below
his nearest neighbour, and wherever he does
not command he must obey. Existing moralities,
accordingly, are mainly fitted to a relation of
command and obedience. Yet command and
obedience are but unfortunate necessities of
human life : society in equality is its normal
state. Already in modern life, and more and
more as it progressively improves, command
and obedience become exceptional facts in life,
equal association its general rule. The morality
of the first ages rested on the obligation to
submit to power ; that of the ages next following,
on the right of the weak to the forbearance and
protection of the strong. How much longer is
one form of society and life to content itself with
the morality made for another? We have had

the morality of submission, and the morality
of chivalry and generosity; the time is now
come for the morality of justice. Whenever,
in former ages, any approach has been made
to society in equality, Justice has asserted its
claims as the foundation of virtue. It was
thus in the free republics of antiquity. But
even in the best of these, the equals were limited
to the free male citizens; slaves, women, and
the unenfranchised residents were under the
law of force. The joint influence of Roman
civilization and of Christianity obliterated these
distinctions, and in theory (if only partially in
practice) declared the claims of the human
being, as such, to be paramount to those of
sex, class, or social position. The barriers which
had begun to be levelled were raised again by
the northern conquests; and the whole of modern
history consists of the slow process by which
they have since been wearing away. We are
entering into an order of things in which justice
will again be the primary virtue; grounded as
before on equal, but now also on sympathetic
association; having its root no longer in the
instinct of equals for self-protection, but in a
cultivated sympathy between them; and no one
being now left out, but an equal measure being
extended to all. It is no novelty that mankind
do not distinctly foresee their own changes,

and that their sentiments are adapted to past, not to coming ages. To see the futurity of the species has always been the privilege of the intellectual élite, or of those who have learnt from them; to have the feelings of that futurity has been the distinction, and usually the martyrdom, of a still rarer élite. Institutions, books, education, society, all go on training human beings for the old, long after the new has come; much more when it is only coming. But the true virtue of human beings is fitness to live together as equals; claiming nothing for themselves but what they as freely concede to every one else; regarding command of any kind as an exceptional necessity, and in all cases a temporary one; and preferring, whenever possible, the society of those with whom leading and following can be alternate and reciprocal. To these virtues, nothing in life as at present constituted gives cultivation by exercise. The family is a school of despotism, in which the virtues of despotism, but also its vices, are largely nourished. Citizenship, in free countries, is partly a school of society in equality; but citizenship fills only a small place in modern life, and does not come near the daily habits or inmost sentiments. The family, justly constituted, would be the real school of the virtues of freedom. It is sure to be a sufficient one of everything else. It will always be a school of obedience for the children, of command for the parents. What is needed is, that it should be a school of sympathy in equality, of living together in love, without power on one side or obedience on the other. This it ought to be between the parents. It would then be an exercise of those virtues which each requires to fit them for all other association, and a model to the children of the feelings and conduct which their temporary training by means of obedience is designed to render habitual, and therefore natural, to them. The moral training of mankind will never be adapted to the conditions of the life for which all other human progress is a preparation, until they practise in the family the same moral rule which is adapted to the normal constitution of human society. Any sentiment of freedom which can exist in a man whose nearest and dearest intimacies are with those of whom he is absolute master, is not the genuine or Christian love of freedom, but, what the love of freedom generally was in the ancients and in the middle ages—an intense feeling of the dignity and importance of his own personality; making him disdain a yoke for himself, of which he has no abhorrence whatever in the abstract, but which he is abundantly ready to impose on others for his own interest or glorification.

I readily admit (and it is the very foundation of my hopes) that numbers of married people even under the present law, (in the higher classes of England probably a great majority,) live in the spirit of a just law of equality. Laws never would be improved, if there were not numerous persons whose moral sentiments are better than the existing laws. Such persons ought to support the principles here advocated; of which the only object is to make all other married couples similar to what these are now. But persons even of considerable moral worth, unless they are also thinkers, are very ready to believe that laws or practices, the evils of which they have not personally experienced, do not produce any evils, but (if seeming to be generally approved of) probably do good, and that it is wrong to object to them. It would, however, be a great mistake in such married people to suppose, because the legal conditions of the tie which unites them do not occur to their thoughts once in a twelvemonth, and because they live and feel in all respects as if they were legally equals, that the same is the case with all other married couples, wherever the husband is not a notorious ruffian. To suppose this, would be to show equal ignorance of human nature and of fact. The less fit a man is for the possession of power—the less likely to be allowed to exercise it over any person with that person's voluntary consent—the more does he hug himself in the consciousness of the power the law gives him, exact its legal rights to the utmost point which custom (the custom of men like himself) will tolerate, and take pleasure in using the power, merely to enliven the agreeable sense of possessing it. What is more; in the most naturally brutal and morally uneducated part of the lower classes, the legal slavery of the woman, and something in the merely physical subjection to their will as an instrument, causes them to feel a sort of disrespect and contempt towards their own wife which they do not feel towards any other woman, or any other human being, with whom they come in contact; and which makes her seem to them an appropriate subject for any kind of indignity. Let an acute observer of the signs of feeling, who has the requisite opportunities, judge for himself whether this is not the case: and if he finds that it is, let him not wonder at any amount of disgust and indignation that can be felt against institutions which lead naturally to this depraved state of the human mind.

We shall be told, perhaps, that religion imposes the duty of obedience; as every established fact which is too bad to admit of any other defence, is always presented to us as an injunction of religion. The Church, it is very true, enjoins it in her formularies, but it would be difficult to derive any such injunction from Christianity. We are told that St. Paul said, " Wives, obey your husbands :" but he also said, " Slaves, obey your masters." It was not St. Paul's business, nor was it consistent with his object, the propagation of Christianity, to incite any one to rebellion against existing laws. The apostle's acceptance of all social institutions as he found them, is no more to be construed as a disapproval of attempts to improve them at the proper time, than his declaration, " The powers that be are ordained of God," gives his sanction to military despotism, and to that alone, as the Christian form of political government, or commands passive obedience to it. To pretend that Christianity was intended to stereotype existing forms of government and society, and protect them against change, is to reduce it to the level of Islamism or of Brahminism. It is precisely because Christianity has not done this, that it has been the religion of the progressive portion of mankind, and Islamism, Brahminism, &c., have been those of the stationary portions ; or rather (for there is no such thing as a really stationary society) of the declining portions. There have been abundance of people, in all ages of Christianity, who tried to make it something of the same kind ; to convert us into a sort of Christian

Mussulmans, with the Bible for a Koran, prohi-
biting all improvement: and great has been their
power, and many have had to sacrifice their lives
in resisting them. But they have been resisted,
and the resistance has made us what we are, and
will yet make us what we are to be.

After what has been said respecting the obligation of obedience, it is almost superfluous to
say anything concerning the more special point
included in the general one—a woman's right
to her own property; for I need not hope that
this treatise can make any impression upon those
who need anything to convince them that a
woman's inheritance or gains ought to be as
much her own after marriage as before. The
rule is simple : whatever would be the husband's
or wife's if they were not married, should be
under their exclusive control during marriage;
which need not interfere with the power to tie
up property by settlement, in order to preserve
it for children. Some people are sentimentally
shocked at the idea of a separate interest in
money matters, as inconsistent with the ideal
fusion of two lives into one. For my own part,
I am one of the strongest supporters of community
of goods, when resulting from an entire unity of
feeling in the owners, which makes all things
common between them. But I have no relish
for a community of goods resting on the doc-

trine, that what is mine is yours but what is yours is not mine ; and I should prefer to decline entering into such a compact with any one, though I were myself the person to profit by it.

This particular injustice and oppression to women, which is, to common apprehensions, more obvious than all the rest, admits of remedy without interfering with any other mischiefs : and there can be little doubt that it will be one of the earliest remedied. Already, in many of the new and several of the old States of the American Confederation, provisions have been inserted even in the written Constitutions, securing to women equality of rights in this respect : and thereby improving materially the position, in the marriage relation, of those women at least who have property, by leaving them one instrument of power which they have not signed away ; and preventing also the scandalous abuse of the marriage institution, which is perpetrated when a man entraps a girl into marrying him without a settlement, for the sole purpose of getting possession of her money. When the support of the family depends, not on property, but on earnings, the common arrangement, by which the man earns the income and the wife superintends the domestic expenditure, seems to me in general the most suitable division of labour between the two persons. If, in addition to the physical suffering of bearing children, and the whole responsibility of their care and education in early years, the wife undertakes the careful and economical application of the husband's earnings to the general comfort of the family; she takes not only her fair share, but usually the larger share, of the bodily and mental exertion required by their joint existence. If she undertakes any additional portion, it seldom relieves her from this, but only prevents her from performing it properly. The care which she is herself disabled from taking of the children and the household, nobody else takes; those of the children who do not die, grow up as they best can, and the management of the household is likely to be so bad, as even in point of economy to be a great drawback from the value of the wife's earnings. In an otherwise just state of things, it is not, therefore, I think, a desirable custom, that the wife should contribute by her labour to the income of the family. In an unjust state of things, her doing so may be useful to her, by making her of more value in the eyes of the man who is legally her master; but, on the other hand, it enables him still farther to abuse his power, by forcing her to work, and leaving the support of the family to her exertions, while he spends most of his time in drink-

ing and idleness. The *power* of earning is essential to the dignity of a woman, if she has not
independent property. But if marriage were an
equal contract, not implying the obligation of
obedience; if the connexion were no longer enforced to the oppression of those to whom it is
purely a mischief, but a separation, on just
terms (I do not now speak of a divorce), could
be obtained by any woman who was morally
entitled to it; and if she would then find all
honourable employments as freely open to her as
to men; it would not be necessary for her protection, that during marriage she should make
this particular use of her faculties. Like a man
when he chooses a profession, so, when a woman
marries, it may in general be understood that
she makes choice of the management of a household, and the bringing up of a family, as the
first call upon her exertions, during as many
years of her life as may be required for the purpose; and that she renounces, not all other objects and occupations, but all which are not
consistent with the requirements of this. The
actual exercise, in a habitual or systematic
manner, of outdoor occupations, or such as
cannot be carried on at home, would by this
principle be practically interdicted to the greater
number of married women. But the utmost
latitude ought to exist for the adaptation of

general rules to individual suitabilities; and there ought to be nothing to prevent faculties exceptionally adapted to any other pursuit, from obeying their vocation notwithstanding marriage: due provision being made for supplying otherwise any falling-short which might become inevitable, in her full performance of the ordinary functions of mistress of a family. These things, if once opinion were rightly directed on the subject, might with perfect safety be left to be regulated by opinion, without any interference of law.

CHAPTER III.

ON the other point which is involved in the just equality of women, their admissibility to all the functions and occupations hitherto retained as the monopoly of the stronger sex, I should anticipate no difficulty in convincing any one who has gone with me on the subject of the equality of women in the family. I believe that their disabilities elsewhere are only clung to in order to maintain their subordination in domestic life; because the generality of the male sex cannot yet tolerate the idea of living with an equal. Were it not for that, I think that almost every one, in the existing state of opinion in politics and political economy, would admit the injustice of excluding half the human race from the greater number of lucrative occupations, and from almost all high social functions; ordaining from their birth either that they are not, and cannot by any possibility become, fit for employments which are legally open to the stupidest and basest of the other sex, or else that however fit they may be, those employments shall be interdicted to them, in order to be preserved for the exclusive benefit of males. In the last two centuries, when (which was seldom the case) any reason beyond the mere existence of the fact was thought to be required to justify the disabilities of women, people seldom assigned as a reason their inferior mental capacity; which, in times when there was a real trial of personal faculties (from which all women were not excluded) in the struggles of public life, no one really believed in. The reason given in those days was not women's unfitness, but the interest of society, by which was meant the interest of men : just as the *raison d'état*, meaning the convenience of the government, and the support of existing authority, was deemed a sufficient explanation and excuse for the most flagitious crimes. In the present day, power holds a smoother language, and whomsoever it oppresses, always pretends to do so for their own good : accordingly, when anything is forbidden to women, it is thought necessary to say, and desirable to believe, that they are incapable of doing it, and that they depart from their real path of success and happiness when they aspire to it. But to make this reason plausible (I do not say valid), those by whom it is urged must be prepared to carry it to a much greater length than any one ventures to do in the face of present experience. It is not sufficient to maintain that women on the average are less gifted than men on the average, with certain of the higher mental faculties, or that a smaller number of women than of men are fit for occupations and functions of the highest intellectual character. It is necessary to maintain that no women at all are fit for them, and that the most eminent women are inferior in mental faculties to the most mediocre of the men on whom those functions at present devolve. For if the performance of the function is decided either by competition, or by any mode of choice which secures regard to the public interest, there needs be no apprehension that any important employments will fall into the hands of women inferior to average men, or to the average of their male competitors. The only result would be that there would be fewer women than men in such employments; a result certain to happen in any case, if only from the preference always likely to be felt by the majority of women for the one vocation in which there is nobody to compete with them. Now, the most determined depreciator of women will not venture to deny, that when we add the experience of recent times to that of ages past, women, and not a few merely, but many women, have proved themselves capable of everything, perhaps without a single exception, which is done by men, and of doing it successfully and creditably. The utmost that can be said is, that there are many things which none of them have succeeded in doing as well as they have been done by some men—many in which they have not reached the very highest rank. But there are extremely few, dependent only on mental faculties, in which they have not attained the rank next to the highest. Is not this enough, and much more than enough, to make it a tyranny to them, and a detriment to society, that they should not be allowed to compete with men for the exercise of these functions? Is it not a mere truism to say, that such functions are often filled by men far less fit for them than numbers of women, and who would be beaten by women in any fair field of competition? What difference does it make that there may be men somewhere, fully employed about other things, who may be still better qualified for the things in question than these women? Does not this take place in all competitions? Is there so great a superfluity of men fit for high duties, that society can afford to reject the service of any competent person? Are we so certain of always finding a man made to our hands for any duty or function of social importance which falls vacant, that we lose nothing by putting a ban upon one-half of mankind, and refusing beforehand to make their faculties available, however distinguished they may be? And even if we could do without them, would it be consistent with justice to refuse to them their fair share of honour and distinction, or to deny to them the equal moral right of all human beings to choose their occupation (short of injury to others) according to their own preferences, at their own risk? Nor is the injustice confined to them : it is shared by those who are in a position to benefit by their services. To ordain that any kind of persons shall not be physicians, or shall not be advocates, or shall not be members of parliament, is to injure not them only, but all who employ physicians or advocates, or elect members of parliament, and who are deprived of the stimulating effect of greater competition on the exertions of the competitors, as well as restricted to a narrower range of individual choice.

It will perhaps be sufficient if I confine myself, in the details of my argument, to functions of a public nature : since, if I am successful as to those, it probably will be readily granted that women should be admissible to all other occupations to which it is at all material whether they are admitted or not. And here let me begin by marking out one function, broadly distinguished from all others, their right to which is entirely independent of any question which can be raised concerning their faculties. I mean the suffrage, both parliamentary and municipal. The right to share in the choice of those who are to exercise a public trust, is altogether a distinct thing from that of competing for the trust itself. If no one could vote for a member of parliament who was not fit to be a candidate, the government would be a narrow oligarchy indeed. To have a voice in choosing those by whom one is to be governed, is a means of self-protection due to every one, though he were to remain for ever excluded from the function of governing : and that women are considered fit to have such a choice, may be presumed from the fact, that the law already gives it to women in the most important of all cases to themselves : for the choice of the man who is to govern a woman to the end of life, is always supposed to be voluntarily made by herself. In the case of election to public trusts, it is the business of constitutional law to surround the right of suffrage with all needful securities and limitations; but whatever securities are sufficient in the case of the male sex, no others need be required in the case of women. Under whatever conditions, and within whatever limits, men are admitted to the suffrage, there is not a shadow of justification for not admitting women under the same. The majority of the women of any class are not likely to differ in political opinion from the majority of the men of the same class, unless the question be one in which the interests of women, as such, are in some way involved; and if they are so, women require the suffrage, as their guarantee of just and equal consideration. This ought to be obvious even to those who coincide in no other of the doctrines for which I contend. Even if every woman were a wife, and if every wife ought to be a slave, all the more would these slaves stand in need of legal protection: and we know what legal protection the slaves have, where the laws are made by their masters.

With regard to the fitness of women, not only to participate in elections, but themselves to hold offices or practise professions involving important public responsibilities; I have already observed that this consideration is not essential to the practical question in dispute: since any woman, who succeeds in an open profession, proves by that very fact that she is qualified for it. And in the case of public offices, if the political system of the country is such as to exclude unfit men, it will equally exclude unfit women: while if it is not, there is no additional evil in the fact that the unfit persons whom it admits may be either women or men. As long therefore as it is acknowledged that even a few women may be fit for these duties, the laws which shut the door on those exceptions cannot be justified by any opinion which can be held respecting the capacities of women in general. But, though this last consideration is not essential, it is far from being irrelevant. An unprejudiced view of it gives additional strength to the arguments against the disabilities of women, and reinforces them by high considerations of practical utility.

Let us at first make entire abstraction of all psychological considerations tending to show, that any of the mental differences supposed to exist between women and men are but the natural effect of the differences in their education and circumstances, and indicate no radical difference, far less radical inferiority, of nature. Let us consider women only as they already are, or as they are known to have been ; and the capacities which they have already practically shown. What they have done, that at least, if nothing else, it is proved that they can do. When we consider how sedulously they are all trained away from, instead of being trained towards, any of the occupations or objects reserved for men, it is evident that I am taking a very humble ground for them, when I rest their case on what they have actually achieved. For, in this case, negative evidence is worth little, while any positive evidence is conclusive. It cannot be inferred to be impossible that a woman should be a Homer, or an Aristotle, or a Michael Angelo, or a Beethoven, because no woman has yet actually produced works comparable to theirs in any of those lines of excellence. This negative fact at most leaves the question uncertain, and open to psychological discussion. But it is quite certain that a woman can be a Queen Elizabeth, or a Deborah, or a Joan of Arc, since this is not inference, but fact. Now it is a curious consideration, that the only things which the existing law excludes women from doing, are the things which they have proved that they are able to do. There is no law to prevent a woman from having written all the plays of Shakspeare, or composed all the operas of Mozart. But Queen Elizabeth or Queen Victoria, had they not inherited the throne, could not have been intrusted with the smallest of the political duties, of which the former showed herself equal to the greatest.

If anything conclusive could be inferred from experience, without psychological analysis, it would be that the things which women are not allowed to do are the very ones for which they are peculiarly qualified; since their vocation for government has made its way, and become conspicuous, through the very few opportunities which have been given; while in the lines of distinction which apparently were freely open to them, they have by no means so eminently distinguished themselves. We know how small a number of reigning queens history presents, in

comparison with that of kings. Of this smaller
number a far larger proportion have shown
talents for rule; though many of them have
occupied the throne in difficult periods. It is
remarkable, too, that they have, in a great
number of instances, been distinguished by merits
the most opposite to the imaginary and conventional character of women: they have been as
much remarked for the firmness and vigour of
their rule, as for its intelligence. When, to
queens and empresses, we add regents, and vice-
roys of provinces, the list of women who have
been eminent rulers of mankind swells to a great
length.* This fact is so undeniable, that some
one, long ago, tried to retort the argument, and
turned the admitted truth into an additional
insult, by saying that queens are better than

* Especially is this true if we take into consideration Asia
as well as Europe. If a Hindoo principality is strongly, vigi-
lantly, and economically governed; if order is preserved without
oppression; if cultivation is extending, and the people prosperous,
in three cases out of four that principality is under a woman's
rule. This fact, to me an entirely unexpected one, I have collected from a long official knowledge of Hindoo governments.
There are many such instances: for though, by Hindoo institutions,
a woman cannot reign, she is the legal regent of a kingdom during
the minority of the heir ; and minorities are frequent, the lives of
the male rulers being so often prematurely terminated through
the effect of inactivity and sensual excesses. When we consider
that these princesses have never been seen in public, have never
conversed with any man not of their own family except from behind a curtain, that they do not read, and if they did, there is no
book in their languages which can give them the smallest instruction on political affairs; the example they afford of the natural capacity of women for government is very striking.

kings, because under kings women govern, but under queens, men.

It may seem a waste of reasoning to argue against a bad joke; but such things do affect people's minds; and I have heard men quote this saying, with an air as if they thought that there was something in it. At any rate, it will serve as well as anything else for a starting point in discussion. I say, then, that it is not true that under kings, women govern. Such cases are entirely exceptional: and weak kings have quite as often governed ill through the influence of male favourites, as of female. When a king is governed by a woman merely through his amatory propensities, good government is not probable, though even then there are exceptions. But French history counts two kings who have voluntarily given the direction of affairs during many years, the one to his mother, the other to his sister: one of them, Charles VIII., was a mere boy, but in doing so he followed the intentions of his father Louis XI., the ablest monarch of his age. The other, Saint Louis, was the best, and one of the most vigorous rulers, since the time of Charlemagne. Both these princesses ruled in a manner hardly equalled by any prince among their cotemporaries. The emperor Charles the Fifth, the most politic prince of his time, who had as great a number of able men in his service as a ruler ever had, and was one of the least likely of all sovereigns to sacrifice his interest to personal feelings, made two princesses of his family successively Governors of the Netherlands, and kept one or other of them in that post during his whole life, (they were afterwards succeeded by a third). Both ruled very successfully, and one of them, Margaret of Austria, was one of the ablest politicians of the age. So much for one side of the question. Now as to the other. When it is said that under queens men govern, is the same meaning to be understood as when kings are said to be governed by women? Is it meant that queens choose as their instruments of government, the associates of their personal pleasures? The case is rare even with those who are as unscrupulous on the latter point as Catherine II.: and it is not in these cases that the good government, alleged to arise from male influence, is to be found. If it be true, then, that the administration is in the hands of better men under a queen than under an average king, it must be that queens have a superior capacity for choosing them; and women must be better qualified than men both for the position of sovereign, and for that of chief minister; for the principal business of a prime minister is not to govern in person, but to find the fittest persons to conduct every department of public affairs.

The more rapid insight into character, which
is one of the admitted points of superiority
in women over men, must certainly make them,
with anything like parity of qualifications in
other respects, more apt than men in that choice
of instruments, which is nearly the most important business of every one who has to do with
governing mankind. Even the unprincipled
Catherine de' Medici could feel the value of a
Chancellor de l'Hôpital. But it is also true
that most great queens have been great by their
own talents for government, and have been
well served precisely for that reason. They
retained the supreme direction of affairs in their
own hands : and if they listened to good advisers,
they gave by that fact the strongest proof that
their judgment fitted them for dealing with the
great questions of government.

Is it reasonable to think that those who are
fit for the greater functions of politics, are incapable of qualifying themselves for the less?
Is there any reason in the nature of things, that
the wives and sisters of princes should, whenever
called on, be found as competent as the princes
themselves to *their* business, but that the wives
and sisters of statesmen, and administrators, and
directors of companies, and managers of public
institutions, should be unable to do what is done
by their brothers and husbands? The real

reason is plain enough; it is that princesses, being more raised above the generality of men by their rank than placed below them by their sex, have never been taught that it was improper for them to concern themselves with politics; but have been allowed to feel the liberal interest natural to any cultivated human being, in the great transactions which took place around them, and in which they might be called on to take a part. The ladies of reigning families are the only women who are allowed the same range of interests and freedom of development as men; and it is precisely in their case that there is not found to be any inferiority. Exactly where and in proportion as women's capacities for government have been tried, in that proportion have they been found adequate.

This fact is in accordance with the best general conclusions which the world's imperfect experience seems as yet to suggest, concerning the peculiar tendencies and aptitudes characteristic of women, as women have hitherto been. I do not say, as they will continue to be; for, as I have already said more than once, I consider it presumption in any one to pretend to decide what women are or are not, can or cannot be, by natural constitution. They have always hitherto been kept, as far as regards spontaneous development, in so unnatural a state, that their nature cannot but have been greatly distorted and disguised ; and no one can safely pronounce that if women's nature were left to choose its direction as freely as men's, and if no artificial bent were attempted to be given to it except that required by the conditions of human society, and given to both sexes alike, there would be any material difference, or perhaps any difference at all, in the character and capacities which would unfold themselves. I shall presently show, that even the least contestable of the differences which now exist, are such as may very well have been produced merely by circumstances, without any difference of natural capacity. But, looking at women as they are known in experience, it may be said of them, with more truth than belongs to most other generalizations on the subject, that the general bent of their talents is towards the practical. This statement is conformable to all the public history of women, in the present and the past. It is no less borne out by common and daily experience. Let us consider the special nature of the mental capacities most characteristic of a woman of talent. They are all of a kind which fits them for practice, and makes them tend towards it. What is meant by a woman's capacity of intuitive perception ? It means, a rapid and correct insight into present fact. It has nothing to do with general prin-

ciples. Nobody ever perceived a scientific law
of nature by intuition, nor arrived at a general
rule of duty or prudence by it. These are
results of slow and careful collection and comparison of experience ; and neither the men nor
the women of intuition usually shine in this department, unless, indeed, the experience necessary
is such as they can acquire by themselves. For
what is called their intuitive sagacity makes
them peculiarly apt in gathering such general
truths as can be collected from their individual
means of observation. When, consequently, they
chance to be as well provided as men are with
the results of other people's experience, by
reading and education, (I use the word chance
advisedly, for, in respect to the knowledge that
tends to fit them for the greater concerns of
life, the only educated women are the self-
educated) they are better furnished than men
in general with the essential requisites of skilful
and successful practice. Men who have been
much taught, are apt to be deficient in the
sense of present fact; they do not see, in the
facts which they are called upon to deal with,
what is really there, but what they have been
taught to expect. This is seldom the case with
women of any ability. Their capacity of " intuition " preserves them from it. With equality
of experience and of general faculties, a woman

usually sees much more than a man of what
is immediately before her. Now this sensibility
to the present, is the main quality on which the
capacity for practice, as distinguished from theory,
depends. To discover general principles, belongs
to the speculative faculty : to discern and dis-
criminate the particular cases in which they are
and are not applicable, constitutes practical talent :
and for this, women as they now are have a
peculiar aptitude. I admit that there can be
no good practice without principles, and that
the predominant place which quickness of observation holds among a woman's faculties, makes
her particularly apt to build over-hasty generalizations upon her own observation ; though at
the same time no less ready in rectifying those
generalizations, as her observation takes a wider
range. But the corrective to this defect, is access
to the experience of the human race ; general
knowledge—exactly the thing which education
can best supply. A woman's mistakes are specifically those of a clever self-educated man, who
often sees what men trained in routine do not
see, but falls into errors for want of knowing
things which have long been known. Of course
he has acquired much of the pre-existing knowledge, or he could not have got on at all ; but
what he knows of it he has picked up in frag-
ments and at random, as women do.

But this gravitation of women's minds to
the present, to the real, to actual fact, while
in its exclusiveness it is a source of errors, is
also a most useful counteractive of the contrary
error. The principal and most characteristic
aberration of speculative minds as such, consists
precisely in the deficiency of this lively perception and ever-present sense of objective fact.
For want of this, they often not only overlook
the contradiction which outward facts oppose
to their theories, but lose sight of the legitimate purpose of speculation altogether, and let
their speculative faculties go astray into regions
not peopled with real beings, animate or inani-
mate, even idealized, but with personified shadows
created by the illusions of metaphysics or by the
mere entanglement of words, and think these
shadows the proper objects of the highest, the most
transcendant, philosophy. Hardly anything can
be of greater value to a man of theory and
speculation who employs himself not in col-
lecting materials of knowledge by observation,
but in working them up by processes of thought
into comprehensive truths of science and laws of
conduct, than to carry on his speculations in the
companionship, and under the criticism, of a really
superior woman. There is nothing comparable
to it for keeping his thoughts within the limits
of real things, and the actual facts of nature.

A woman seldom runs wild after an abstraction. The habitual direction of her mind to dealing with things as individuals rather than in groups, and (what is closely connected with it) her more lively interest in the present feelings of persons, which makes her consider first of all, in anything which claims to be applied to practice, in what manner persons will be affected by it—these two things make her extremely unlikely to put faith in any speculation which loses sight of individuals, and deals with things as if they existed for the benefit of some imaginary entity, some mere creation of the mind, not resolvable into the feelings of living beings. Women's thoughts are thus as useful in giving reality to those of thinking men, as men's thoughts in giving width and largeness to those of women. In depth, as distinguished from breadth, I greatly doubt if even now, women, compared with men, are at any disadvantage.

If the existing mental characteristics of women are thus valuable even in aid of speculation, they are still more important, when speculation has done its work, for carrying out the results of speculation into practice. For the reasons already given, women are comparatively unlikely to fall into the common error of men, that of sticking to their rules in a case whose specialities either take it out of the class to which the rules are applicable, or require a special adaptation of them. Let us now consider another of the admitted superiorities of clever women, greater quickness of apprehension. Is not this pre-eminently a quality which fits a person for practice? In action, everything continually depends upon deciding promptly. In specula-tion, nothing does. A mere thinker can wait, can take time to consider, can collect additional evidence; he is not obliged to complete his philosophy at once, lest the opportunity should go by. The power of drawing the best con-clusion possible from insufficient data is not indeed useless in philosophy; the construction of a provisional hypothesis consistent with all known facts is often the needful basis for further inquiry. But this faculty is rather serviceable in philosophy, than the main qualification for it: and, for the auxiliary as well as for the main operation, the philosopher can allow himself any time he pleases. He is in no need of the capa-city of doing rapidly what he does; what he rather needs is patience, to work on slowly until imper-fect lights have become perfect, and a conjecture has ripened into a theorem. For those, on the contrary, whose business is with the fugitive and perishable—with individual facts, not kinds of facts—rapidity of thought is a qualification next only in importance to the power of thought itself.

He who has not his faculties under immediate command, in the contingencies of action, might as well not have them at all. He may be fit to criticize, but he is not fit to act. Now it is in this that women, and the men who are most like women, confessedly excel. The other sort of man, however pre-eminent may be his faculties, arrives slowly at complete command of them: rapidity of judgment and promptitude of judicious action, even in the things he knows best, are the gradual and late result of strenuous effort grown into habit.

It will be said, perhaps, that the greater nervous susceptibility of women is a disqualification for practice, in anything but domestic life, by rendering them mobile, changeable, too vehemently under the influence of the moment, incapable of dogged perseverance, unequal and uncertain in the power of using their faculties. I think that these phrases sum up the greater part of the objections commonly made to the fitness of women for the higher class of serious business. Much of all this is the mere overflow of nervous energy run to waste, and would cease when the energy was directed to a definite end. Much is also the result of conscious or unconscious cultivation; as we see by the almost total disappearance of " hysterics " and fainting fits, since they have gone out of fashion. More-

over, when people are brought up, like many
women of the higher classes (though less so in
our own country than in any other) a kind of hot-
house plants, shielded from the wholesome vicissi-
tudes of air and temperature, and untrained in
any of the occupations and exercises which give
stimulus and development to the circulatory and
muscular system, while their nervous system,
especially in its emotional department, is kept in
unnaturally active play; it is no wonder if those
of them who do not die of consumption, grow
up with constitutions liable to derangement from
slight causes, both internal and external, and
without stamina to support any task, physical or
mental, requiring continuity of effort. But
women brought up to work for their liveli-
hood show none of these morbid characteristics,
unless indeed they are chained to an excess of
sedentary work in confined and unhealthy rooms.
Women who in their early years have shared in
the healthful physical education and bodily freedom of their brothers, and who obtain a suffi-
ciency of pure air and exercise in after-life, very
rarely have any excessive susceptibility of nerves
which can disqualify them for active pursuits.
There is indeed a certain proportion of persons,
in both sexes, in whom an unusual degree of
nervous sensibility is constitutional, and of so
marked a character as to be the feature of their

organization which exercises the greatest influence over the whole character of the vital phenomena. This constitution, like other physical conformations, is hereditary, and is transmitted to sons as well as daughters; but it is possible, and probable, that the nervous temperament (as it is called) is inherited by a greater number of women than of men. We will assume this as a fact: and let me then ask, are men of nervous temperament found to be unfit for the duties and pursuits usually followed by men? If not, why should women of the same temperament be unfit for them? The peculiarities of the temperament are, no doubt, within certain limits, an obstacle to success in some employments, though an aid to it in others. But when the occupation is suitable to the temperament, and sometimes even when it is unsuitable, the most brilliant examples of success are continually given by the men of high nervous sensibility. They are distinguished in their practical manifestations chiefly by this, that being susceptible of a higher degree of excitement than those of another physical constitution, their powers when excited differ more than in the case of other people, from those shown in their ordinary state: they are raised, as it were, above themselves, and do things with ease which they are wholly incapable of at other times. But this lofty excitement is not, except in weak bodily constitutions, a mere flash, which passes away immediately, leaving no perm. ?ent traces, and incompatible with persistent and steady pursuit of an object. It is the character of the nervous temperament to be capable of *sustained* excitement, holding out through long continued efforts. It is what is meant by *spirit*. It is what makes the high-bred racehorse run without slackening speed till he drops down dead. It is what has enabled so many delicate women to maintain the most sublime constancy not only at the stake, but through a long preliminary succession of mental and bodily tortures. It is evident that people of this temperament are particularly apt for what may be called the executive department of the leadership of mankind. They are the material of great orators, great preachers, impressive diffusers of moral influences. Their constitution might be deemed less favourable to the qualities required from a statesman in the cabinet, or from a judge. It would be so, if the consequence necessarily followed that because people are excitable they must always be in a state of excitement. But this is wholly a question of training. Strong feeling is the instrument and element of strong self-control : but it requires to be cultivated in that direction. When it is, it forms not the heroes of impulse only, but those also of self-conquest. History and experience prove that

the most passionate characters are the most fana-
tically rigid in their feelings of duty, when their
passion has been trained to act in that direction.
The judge who gives a just decision in a case
where his feelings are intensely interested on the
other side, derives from that same strength of
feeling the determined sense of the obligation of
justice, which enables him to achieve this victory
over himself. The capability of that lofty enthusiasm which takes the human being out of
his every-day character, reacts upon the daily
character itself. His aspirations and powers when
he is in this exceptional state, become the type
with which he compares, and by which he esti-
mates, his sentiments and proceedings at other
times: and his habitual purposes assume a character moulded by and assimilated to the moments of lofty excitement, although those, from
the physical nature of a human being, can only
be transient. Experience of races, as well as of
individuals, does not show those of excitable temperament to be less fit, on the average, either
for speculation or practice, than the more unex-
citable. The French, and the Italians, are un-
doubtedly by nature more nervously excitable
than the Teutonic races, and, compared at least
with the English, they have a much greater
habitual and daily emotional life: but have they
been less great in science, in public business, in

legal and judicial eminence, or in war? There
is abundant evidence that the Greeks were of
old, as their descendants and successors still are,
one of the most excitable of the races of mankind. It is superfluous to ask, what among the
achievements of men they did not excel in. The
Romans, probably, as an equally southern people,
had the same original temperament: but the
stern character of their national discipline, like
that of the Spartans, made them an example of
the opposite type of national character; the
greater strength of their natural feelings being
chiefly apparent in the intensity which the same
original temperament made it possible to give to
the artificial. If these cases exemplify what a
naturally excitable people may be made, the Irish
Celts afford one of the aptest examples of what
they are when left to themselves; (if those can
be said to be left to themselves who have been
for centuries under the indirect influence of bad
government, and the direct training of a Catholic
hierarchy and of a sincere belief in the Catholic
religion.) The Irish character must be considered,
therefore, as an unfavourable case: yet, whenever
the circumstances of the individual have been at
all favourable, what people have shown greater
capacity for the most varied and multifarious individual eminence? Like the French compared
with the English, the Irish with the Swiss, the

Greeks or Italians compared with the German races, so women compared with men may be found, on the average, to do the same things with some variety in the particular kind of excellence. But, that they would do them fully as well on the whole, if their education and cultivation were adapted to correcting instead of aggravating the infirmities incident to their temperament, I see not the smallest reason to doubt.

Supposing it, however, to be true that women's minds are by nature more mobile than those of men, less capable of persisting long in the same continuous effort, more fitted for dividing their faculties among many things than for travelling in any one path to the highest point which can be reached by it : this may be true of women as they now are (though not without great and numerous exceptions), and may account for their having remained behind the highest order of men in precisely the things in which this absorption of the whole mind in one set of ideas and occupations may seem to be most requisite. Still, this difference is one which can only affect the kind of excellence, not the excellence itself, or its practical worth : and it remains to be shown whether this exclusive working of a part of the mind, this absorption of the whole thinking faculty in a single subject, and concentration of it on a single work, is the normal and healthful condition of the human faculties, even for speculative uses. I believe that what is gained in special development by this concentration, is lost in the capacity of the mind for the other purposes of life; and even in abstract thought, it is my decided opinion that the mind does more by frequently returning to a difficult problem, than by sticking to it without interruption. For the purposes, at all events, of practice, from its highest to its humblest departments, the capacity of passing promptly from one subject of consideration to another, without letting the active spring of the intellect run down between the two, is a power far more valuable; and this power women pre-eminently possess, by virtue of the very mobility of which they are accused. They perhaps have it from nature, but they certainly have it by training and education; for nearly the whole of the occupations of women consist in the management of small but multitudinous details, on each of which the mind cannot dwell even for a minute, but must pass on to other things, and if anything requires longer thought, must steal time at odd moments for thinking of it. The capacity indeed which women show for doing their thinking in circumstances and at times which almost any man would make an excuse to himself for not attempting it, has often been noticed: and a woman's mind, though it may be occupied only with small things, can hardly ever permit itself to be vacant, as a man's so often is when not engaged in what he chooses to consider the business of his life. The business of a woman's ordinary life is things in general, and can as little cease to go on as the world to go round.

But (it is said) there is anatomical evidence of the superior mental capacity of men compared with women : they have a larger brain. I reply, that in the first place the fact itself is doubtful. It is by no means established that the brain of a woman is smaller than that of a man. If it is inferred merely because a woman's bodily frame generally is of less dimensions than a man's, this criterion would lead to strange consequences. A tall and large-boned man must on this showing be wonderfully superior in intelligence to a small man, and an elephant or a whale must prodigiously excel mankind. The size of the brain in human beings, anatomists say, varies much less than the size of the body, or even of the head, and the one cannot be at all inferred from the other. It is certain that some women have as large a brain as any man. It is within my knowledge that a man who had weighed many human brains, said that the heaviest he knew of, heavier even than Cuvier's (the heaviest pre-

viously recorded,) was that of a woman. Next,
I must observe that the precise relation which
exists between the brain and the intellectual
powers is not yet well understood, but is a
subject of great dispute. That there is a very
close relation we cannot doubt. The brain is
certainly the material organ of thought and
feeling: and (making abstraction of the great
unsettled controversy respecting the appropriation
of different parts of the brain to different mental
faculties) I admit that it would be an anomaly,
and an exception to all we know of the general
laws of life and organization, if the size of the
organ were wholly indifferent to the function; if
no accession of power were derived from the
greater magnitude of the instrument. But the
exception and the anomaly would be fully as
great if the organ exercised influence by its
magnitude *only*. In all the more delicate operations of nature—of which those of the animated
creation are the most delicate, and those of the
nervous system by far the most delicate of these
—differences in the effect depend as much on
differences of quality in the physical agents, as
on their quantity: and if the quality of an instrument is to be tested by the nicety and delicacy of the work it can do, the indications point
to a greater average fineness of quality in the
brain and nervous system of women than of men.

Dismissing abstract difference of quality, a thing difficult to verify, the efficiency of an organ is known to depend not solely on its size but on its activity: and of this we have an approximate measure in the energy with which the blood circulates through it, both the stimulus and the reparative force being mainly dependent on the circulation. It would not be surprising—it is indeed an hypothesis which accords well with the differences actually observed between the mental operations of the two sexes—if men on the average should have the advantage in the size of the brain, and women in activity of cerebral circulation. The results which conjecture, founded on analogy, would lead us to expect from this difference of organization, would correspond to some of those which we most commonly see. In the first place, the mental operations of men might be expected to be slower. They would neither be so prompt as women in thinking, nor so quick to feel. Large bodies take more time to get into full action. On the other hand, when once got thoroughly into play, men's brain would bear more work. It would be more persistent in the line first taken; it would have more difficulty in changing from one mode of action to another, but, in the one thing it was doing, it could go on longer without loss of power or sense of fatigue. And do we not find that

the things in which men most excel women are
those which require most plodding and long
hammering at a single thought, while women do
best what must be done rapidly? A woman's
brain is sooner fatigued, sooner exhausted; but
given the degree of exhaustion, we should expect
to find that it would recover itself sooner. I
repeat that this speculation is entirely hypo-
thetical; it pretends to no more than to suggest
a line of enquiry. I have before repudiated the
notion of its being yet certainly known that
there is any natural difference at all in the
average strength or direction of the mental capacities of the two sexes, much less what that
difference is. Nor is it possible that this should
be known, so long as the psychological laws of the
formation of character have been so little studied,
even in a general way, and in the particular
case never scientifically applied at all; so long
as the most obvious external causes of difference
of character are habitually disregarded—left un-
noticed by the observer, and looked down upon
with a kind of supercilious contempt by the
prevalent schools both of natural history and of
mental philosophy: who, whether they look for
the source of what mainly distinguishes human
beings from one another, in the world of matter
or in that of spirit, agree in running down those
who prefer to explain these differences by the

different relations of human beings to society and life.

To so ridiculous an extent are the notions formed of the nature of women, mere empirical generalizations, framed, without philosophy or analysis, upon the first instances which present themselves, that the popular idea of it is different in different countries, according as the opinions and social circumstances of the country have given to the women living in it any speciality of development or non-development. An Oriental thinks that women are by nature peculiarly voluptuous; see the violent abuse of them on this ground in Hindoo writings. An Englishman usually thinks that they are by nature cold. The sayings about women's fickleness are mostly of French origin; from the famous distich of Francis the First, upward and downward. In England it is a common remark, how much more constant women are than men. Inconstancy has been longer reckoned discreditable to a woman, in England than in France; and Englishwomen are besides, in their inmost nature, much more subdued to opinion. It may be remarked by the way, that Englishmen are in peculiarly unfavourable circumstances for attempting to judge what is or is not natural, not merely to women, but to men, or to human beings altogether, at least if they have only English experience to go upon: because there is no place where human nature shows so little of its original lineaments. Both in a good and a bad sense, the English are farther from a state of nature than any other modern people. They are, more than any other people, a product of civilization and discipline. England is the country in which social discipline has most succeeded, not so much in conquering, as in suppressing, whatever is liable to conflict with it. The English, more than any other people, not only act but feel according to rule. In other countries, the taught opinion, or the requirement of society, may be the stronger power, but the promptings of the individual nature are always visible under it, and often resisting it : rule may be stronger than nature, but nature is still there. In England, rule has to a great degree substituted itself for nature. The greater part of life is carried on, not by following inclination under the control of rule, but by having no inclination but that of following a rule. Now this has its good side doubtless, though it has also a wretchedly bad one ; but it must render an Englishman peculiarly ill-qualified to pass a judgment on the original tendencies of human nature from his own experience. The errors to which observers elsewhere are liable on the subject, are of a different character. An Englishman is ignorant respecting human nature, a Frenchman is prejudiced. An Englishman's errors are negative, a Frenchman's positive. An Englishman fancies that things do not exist, because he never sees them; a Frenchman thinks they must always and necessarily exist, because he does see them. An Englishman does not know nature, because he has had no opportunity of observing it; a Frenchman generally knows a great deal of it, but often mistakes it, because he has only seen it sophisticated and distorted. For the artificial state superinduced by society disguises the natural tendencies of the thing which is the subject of observation, in two different ways: by extinguishing the nature, or by transforming it. In the one case there is but a starved residuum of nature remaining to be studied; in the other case there is much, but it may have expanded in any direction rather than that in which it would spontaneously grow.

I have said that it cannot now be known how much of the existing mental differences between men and women is natural, and how much artificial; whether there are any natural differences at all; or, supposing all artificial causes of difference to be withdrawn, what natural character would be revealed. I am not about to attempt what I have pronounced impossible: but doubt does not forbid conjecture, and where certainty is unattainable, there may yet be the means of arriving at some degree of probability. The first point, the origin of the differences actually

observed, is the one most accessible to speculation ; and I shall attempt to approach it, by the
only path by which it can be reached ; by tracing
the mental consequences of external influences.
We cannot isolate a human being from the circumstances of his condition, so as to ascertain ex-
perimentally what he would have been by nature ;
but we can consider what he is, and what his circumstances have been, and whether the one would
have been capable of producing the other.

Let us take, then, the only marked case which
observation affords, of apparent inferiority of
women to men, if we except the merely physical
one of bodily strength. No production in philosophy, science, or art, entitled to the first rank,
has been the work of a woman. Is there any
mode of accounting for this, without supposing
that women are naturally incapable of producing
them ?

In the first place, we may fairly question
whether experience has afforded sufficient grounds
for an induction. It is scarcely three generations
since women, saving very rare exceptions, have
begun to try their capacity in philosophy, science,
or art. It is only in the present generation that
their attempts have been at all numerous ; and
they are even now extremely few, everywhere but
in England and France. It is a relevant question, whether a mind possessing the requisites of

first-rate eminence in speculation or creative art could have been expected, on the mere calculation of chances, to turn up during that lapse of time, among the women whose tastes and personal position admitted of their devoting themselves to these pursuits.   In all things which there has yet been time for—in all but the very highest grades in the scale of excellence, especially in the department in which they have been longest engaged, literature (both prose and poetry)—women have done quite as much, have obtained fully as high prizes and as many of them, as could be expected from the length of time and the number of competitors.   If we go back to the earlier period when very few women made the attempt, yet some of those few made it with distinguished success. The Greeks always accounted Sappho among their great poets; and we may well suppose that Myrtis, said to have been the teacher of Pindar, and Corinna, who five times bore away from him the prize of poetry, must at least have had sufficient merit to admit of being compared with that great name.   Aspasia did not leave any philosophical writings; but it is an admitted fact that Socrates resorted to her for instruction, and avowed himself to have obtained it.

If we consider the works of women in modern times, and contrast them with those of men, either in the literary or the artistic department,

such inferiority as may be observed resolves
itself essentially into one thing : but that is a
most material one ; deficiency of originality. Not
total deficiency ; for every production of mind
which is of any substantive value, has an originality of its own—is a conception of the mind
itself, not a copy of something else. Thoughts
original, in the sense of being unborrowed—of
being derived from the thinker's own observations
or intellectual processes—are abundant in the
writings of women. But they have not yet
produced any of those great and luminous new
ideas which form an era in thought, nor those
fundamentally new conceptions in art, which
open a vista of possible effects not before thought
of, and found a new school. Their compositions
are mostly grounded on the existing fund of
thought, and their creations do not deviate widely
from existing types. This is the sort of inferiority
which their works manifest : for in point of execution, in the detailed application of thought,
and the perfection of style, there is no inferiority.
Our best novelists in point of composition, and
of the management of detail, have mostly been
women ; and there is not in all modern literature
a more eloquent vehicle of thought than the style
of Madame de Stael, nor, as a specimen of purely
artistic excellence, anything superior to the prose
of Madame Sand, whose style acts upon the

nervous system like a symphony of Haydn or Mozart. High originality of conception is, as I have said, what is chiefly wanting. And now to examine if there is any manner in which this deficiency can be accounted for.

Let us remember, then, so far as regards mere thought, that during all that period in the world's existence, and in the progress of cultivation, in which great and fruitful new truths could be arrived at by mere force of genius, with little previous study and accumulation of knowledge—during all that time women did not concern themselves with speculation at all. From the days of Hypatia to those of the Reformation, the illustrious Heloisa is almost the only woman to whom any such achievement might have been possible; and we know not how great a capacity of speculation in her may have been lost to mankind by the misfortunes of her life. Never since any considerable number of women have began to cultivate serious thought, has originality been possible on easy terms. Nearly all the thoughts which can be reached by mere strength of original faculties, have long since been arrived at; and originality, in any high sense of the word, is now scarcely ever attained but by minds which have undergone elaborate discipline, and are deeply versed in the results of previous thinking. It is Mr. Maurice, I think, who has remarked on the present age, that its most original thinkers are those who have known most thoroughly what had been thought by their predecessors: and this will always henceforth be the case. Every fresh stone in the edifice has now to be placed on the top of so many others, that a long process of climbing, and of carrying up materials, has to be gone through by whoever aspires to take a share in the present stage of the work. How many women are there who have gone through any such process? Mrs. Somerville, alone perhaps of women, knows as much of mathematics as is now needful for making any considerable mathematical discovery: is it any proof of inferiority in women, that she has not happened to be one of the two or three persons who in her lifetime have associated their names with some striking advancement of the science? Two women, since political economy has been made a science, have known enough of it to write usefully on the subject: of how many of the innumerable men who have written on it during the same time, is it possible with truth to say more? If no woman has hitherto been a great historian, what woman has had the necessary erudition? If no woman is a great philologist, what woman has studied Sanscrit and Slavonic, the Gothic of Ulphila and the Persic of the Zendavesta? Even in practical matters we all know what is the value of the originality of untaught geniuses. It means, inventing over again in its rudimentary form something already invented and improved upon by many successive inventors. When women have had the preparation which all men now require to be eminently original, it will be time enough to begin judging by experience of their capacity for originality.

It no doubt often happens that a person, who has not widely and accurately studied the thoughts of others on a subject, has by natural sagacity a happy intuition, which he can suggest, but cannot prove, which yet when matured may be an important addition to knowledge : but even then, no justice can be done to it until some other person, who does possess the previous acquirements, takes it in hand, tests it, gives it a scientific or practical form, and fits it into its place among the existing truths of philosophy or science. Is it supposed that such felicitous thoughts do not occur to women ? They occur by hundreds to every woman of intellect. But they are mostly lost, for want of a husband or friend who has the other knowledge which can enable him to estimate them properly and bring them before the world : and even when they are brought before it, they generally appear as his ideas, not their real author's. Who can tell how many of the most original thoughts put forth by male writers, belong to a woman by suggestion, to themselves only by verifying and working out? If I may judge by my own case, a very large proportion indeed.

If we turn from pure speculation to literature in the narrow sense of the term, and the fine arts, there is a very obvious reason why women's literature is, in its general conception and in its main features, an imitation of men's. Why is the Roman literature, as critics proclaim to satiety, not original, but an imitation of the Greek? Simply because the Greeks came first. If women lived in a different country from men, and had never read any of their writings, they would have had a literature of their own. As it is, they have not created one, because they found a highly advanced literature already created. If there had been no suspension of the knowledge of antiquity, or if the Renaissance had occurred before the Gothic cathedrals were built, they never would have been built. We see that, in France and Italy, imitation of the ancient literature stopped the original development even after it had commenced. All women who write are pupils of the great male writers. A painter's early pictures, even if he be a Raffaelle, are undistinguishable in style from those of his master. Even a Mozart does not display his powerful originality in his

133

earliest pieces. What years are to a gifted individual, generations are to a mass. If women's
literature is destined to have a different collective
character from that of men, depending on any
difference of natural tendencies, much longer
time is necessary than has yet elapsed, before it
can emancipate itself from the influence of accepted models, and guide itself by its own impulses. But if, as I believe, there will not prove
to be any natural tendencies common to women,
and distinguishing their genius from that of men,
yet every individual writer among them has her
individual tendencies, which at present are still
subdued by the influence of precedent and example : and it will require generations more, before
their individuality is sufficiently developed to make
head against that influence.

It is in the fine arts, properly so called, that
the *primâ facie* evidence of inferior original
powers in women at first sight appears the
strongest : since opinion (it may be said) does not
exclude them from these, but rather encourages
them, and their education, instead of passing over
this department, is in the affluent classes mainly
composed of it. Yet in this line of exertion they
have fallen still more short than in many others,
of the highest eminence attained by men. This
shortcoming, however, needs no other explanation than the familiar fact, more universally true

in the fine arts than in anything else ; the vast
superiority of professional persons over amateurs.
Women in the educated classes are almost universally taught more or less of some branch or
other of the fine arts, but not that they may gain
their living or their social consequence by it.
Women artists are all amateurs. The exceptions
are only of the kind which confirm the general
truth. Women are taught music, but not for
the purpose of composing, only of executing it :
and accordingly it is only as composers, that
men, in music, are superior to women. The only
one of the fine arts which women do follow, to
any extent, as a profession, and an occupation
for life, is the histrionic ; and in that they are
confessedly equal, if not superior, to men. To
make the comparison fair, it should be made
between the productions of women in any branch
of art, and those of men not following it as a
profession. In musical composition, for example,
women surely have produced fully as good things
as have ever been produced by male amateurs.
There are now a few women, a very few, who
practise painting as a profession, and these are
already beginning to show quite as much talent
as could be expected. Even male painters (*pace*
Mr. Ruskin) have not made any very remarkable
figure these last centuries, and it will be long
before they do so. The reason why the old painters

were so greatly superior to the modern, is that a greatly superior class of men applied themselves to the art. In the fourteenth and fifteenth centuries the Italian painters were the most accomplished men of their age. The greatest of them were men of encyclopædical acquirements and powers, like the great men of Greece. But in their times fine art was, to men's feelings and conceptions, among the grandest things in which a human being could excel; and by it men were made, what only political or military distinction now makes them, the companions of sovereigns, and the equals of the highest nobility. In the present age, men of anything like similar calibre find something more important to do, for their own fame and the uses of the modern world, than painting : and it is only now and then that a Reynolds or a Turner (of whose relative rank among eminent men I do not pretend to an opinion) applies himself to that art. Music belongs to a different order of things ; it does not require the same general powers of mind, but seems more dependant on a natural gift : and it may be thought surprising that no one of the great musical composers has been a woman. But even this natural gift, to be made available for great creations, requires study, and professional devotion to the pursuit. The only countries which have produced first-rate composers, even of the male sex, are Germany and Italy—

countries in which, both in point of special and of general cultivation, women have remained far behind France and England, being generally (it may be said without exaggeration) very little educated, and having scarcely cultivated at all any of the higher faculties of mind. And in those countries the men who are acquainted with the principles of musical composition must be counted by hundreds, or more probably by thousands, the women barely by scores: so that here again, on the doctrine of averages, we cannot reasonably expect to see more than one eminent woman to fifty eminent men; and the last three centuries have not produced fifty eminent male composers either in Germany or in Italy.

There are other reasons, besides those which we have now given, that help to explain why women remain behind men, even in the pursuits which are open to both. For one thing, very few women have time for them. This may seem a paradox; it is an undoubted social fact. The time and thoughts of every woman have to satisfy great previous demands on them for things practical. There is, first, the superintendence of the family and the domestic expenditure, which occupies at least one woman in every family, generally the one of mature years and acquired experience; unless the family is so rich as to admit of delegating that task to hired agency, and submitting to all the

waste and malversation inseparable from that mode
of conducting it. The superintendence of a household, even when not in other respects laborious, is
extremely onerous to the thoughts; it requires
incessant vigilance, an eye which no detail escapes,
and presents questions for consideration and solu-
tion, foreseen and unforeseen, at every hour of the
day, from which the person responsible for them
can hardly ever shake herself free. If a woman
is of a rank and circumstances which relieve her in
a measure from these cares, she has still devolving
on her the management for the whole family of its
intercourse with others—of what is called society,
and the less the call made on her by the former
duty, the greater is always the development of the
latter: the dinner parties, concerts, evening parties,
morning visits, letter writing, and all that goes with
them. All this is over and above the engrossing
duty which society imposes exclusively on women,
of making themselves charming. A clever woman
of the higher ranks finds nearly a sufficient employment of her talents in cultivating the graces
of manner and the arts of conversation. To look
only at the outward side of the subject: the great
and continual exercise of thought which all women
who attach any value to dressing well (I do not
mean expensively, but with taste, and perception
of natural and of artificial *convenance*) must
bestow upon their own dress, perhaps also upon

that of their daughters, would alone go a great
way towards achieving respectable results in art,
or science, or literature, and does actually exhaust
much of the time and mental power they might
have to spare for either.* If it were possible
that all this number of little practical interests
(which are made great to them) should leave
them either much leisure, or much energy and
freedom of mind, to be devoted to art or speculation, they must have a much greater original
supply of active faculty than the vast majority of
men. But this is not all. Independently of the
regular offices of life which devolve upon a woman,
she is expected to have her time and faculties
always at the disposal of everybody. If a man
has not a profession to exempt him from such
demands, still, if he has a pursuit, he offends
nobody by devoting his time to it ; occupation is

* "It appears to be the same right turn of mind which enables
a man to acquire the *truth*, or the just idea of what is right, in
the ornaments, as in the more stable principles of art. It has
still the same centre of perfection, though it is the centre of a
smaller circle.—To illustrate this by the fashion of dress, in
which there is allowed to be a good or bad taste. The component
parts of dress are continually changing from great to little, from
short to long; but the general form still remains : it is still the
same general dress which is comparatively fixed, though on a very
slender foundation; but it is on this which fashion must rest. He who
invents with the most success, or dresses in the best taste, would
probably, from the same sagacity employed to greater purposes,
have discovered equal skill, or have formed the same correct taste,
in the highest labours of art."—*Sir Joshua Reynolds' Discourses*,
Disc. vii.

received as a valid excuse for his not answering to every casual demand which may be made on him. Are a woman's occupations, especially her chosen and voluntary ones, ever regarded as excusing her from any of what are termed the calls of society? Scarcely are her most necessary and recognised duties allowed as an exemption. It requires an illness in the family, or something else out of the common way, to entitle her to give her own business the precedence over other people's amusement. She must always be at the beck and call of somebody, generally of everybody. If she has a study or a pursuit, she must snatch any short interval which accidentally occurs to be employed in it. A celebrated woman, in a work which I hope will some day be published, remarks truly that everything a woman does is done at odd times. Is it wonderful, then, if she does not attain the highest eminence in things which require consecutive attention, and the concentration on them of the chief interest of life? Such is philosophy, and such, above all, is art, in which, besides the devotion of the thoughts and feelings, the hand also must be kept in constant exercise to attain high skill.

There is another consideration to be added to all these. In the various arts and intellectual occupations, there is a degree of proficiency sufficient for living by it, and there is a higher degree on which depend the great productions which immortalize a name. To the attainment of the former, there are adequate motives in the case of all who follow the pursuit professionally : the other is hardly ever attained where there is not, or where there has not been at some period of life, an ardent desire of celebrity. Nothing less is commonly a sufficient stimulus to undergo the long and patient drudgery, which, in the case even of the greatest natural gifts, is absolutely required for great eminence in pursuits in which we already possess so many splendid memorials of the highest genius. Now, whether the cause be natural or artificial, women seldom have this eagerness for fame. Their ambition is generally confined within narrower bounds. The influence they seek is over those who immediately surround them. Their desire is to be liked, loved, or ad-mired, by those whom they see with their eyes : and the proficiency in knowledge, arts, and ac-complishments, which is sufficient for that, almost always contents them. This is a trait of cha-racter which cannot be left out of the account in judging of women as they are. I do not at all believe that it is inherent in women. It is only the natural result of their circumstances. The love of fame in men is encouraged by edu-cation and opinion : to " scorn delights and live laborious days " for its sake, is accounted the part

of "noble minds," even if spoken of as their
"last infirmity," and is stimulated by the access
which fame gives to all objects of ambition, including even the favour of women; while to
women themselves all these objects are closed,
and the desire of fame itself considered daring
and unfeminine. Besides, how could it be that
a woman's interests should not be all concen-
trated upon the impressions made on those who
come into her daily life, when society has ordained that all her duties should be to them, and
has contrived that all her comforts should depend
on them? The natural desire of consideration
from our fellow creatures is as strong in a woman
as in a man; but society has so ordered things
that public consideration is, in all ordinary cases,
only attainable by her through the consideration
of her husband or of her male relations, while
her private consideration is forfeited by making
herself individually prominent, or appearing in
any other character than that of an appendage
to men. Whoever is in the least capable of
estimating the influence on the mind of the
entire domestic and social position and the whole
habit of a life, must easily recognise in that influence a complete explanation of nearly all the
apparent differences between women and men,
including the whole of those which imply any
inferiority.

As for moral differences, considered as distinguished from intellectual, the distinction commonly drawn is to the advantage of women. They are declared to be better than men; an empty compliment, which must provoke a bitter smile from every woman of spirit, since there is no other situation in life in which it is the established order, and considered quite natural and suitable, that the better should obey the worse. If this piece of idle talk is good for anything, it is only as an admission by men, of the corrupting influence of power; for that is certainly the only truth which the fact, if it be a fact, either proves or illustrates. And it *is* true that servitude, except when it actually brutalizes, though corrupting to both, is less so to the slaves than to the slave-masters. It is wholesomer for the moral nature to be restrained, even by arbitrary power, than to be allowed to exercise arbitrary power without restraint. Women, it is said, seldomer fall under the penal law—contribute a much smaller number of offenders to the criminal calendar, than men. I doubt not that the same thing may be said, with the same truth, of negro slaves. Those who are under the control of others cannot often commit crimes, unless at the command and for the purposes of their masters. I do not know a more signal instance of the blindness with which the world, including the

herd of studious men, ignore and pass over all
the influences of social circumstances, than their
silly depreciation of the intellectual, and silly
panegyrics on the moral, nature of women.

The complimentary dictum about women's
superior moral goodness may be allowed to pair
off with the disparaging one respecting their
greater liability to moral bias. Women, we are
told, are not capable of resisting their personal
partialities : their judgment in grave affairs is
warped by their sympathies and antipathies.
Assuming it to be so, it is still to be proved that
women are oftener misled by their personal
feelings than men by their personal interests.
The chief difference would seem in that case to
be, that men are led from the course of duty
and the public interest by their regard for themselves, women (not being allowed to have private
interests of their own) by their regard for somebody else. It is also to be considered, that all
the education which women receive from society
inculcates on them the feeling that the individuals
connected with them are the only ones to whom
they owe any duty—the only ones whose interest
they are called upon to care for ; while, as far as
education is concerned, they are left strangers
even to the elementary ideas which are presup-
posed in any intelligent regard for larger interests or higher moral objects. The complaint

against them resolves itself merely into this, that they fulfil only too faithfully the sole duty which they are taught, and almost the only one which they are permitted to practise.

The concessions of the privileged to the unprivileged are so seldom brought about by any better motive than the power of the unprivileged to extort them, that any arguments against the prerogative of sex are likely to be little attended to by the generality, as long as they are able to say to themselves that women do not complain of it. That fact certainly enables men to retain the unjust privilege some time longer; but does not render it less unjust. Exactly the same thing may be said of the women in the harem of an Oriental: they do not complain of not being allowed the freedom of European women. They think our women insufferably bold and unfeminine. How rarely it is that even men complain of the general order of society; and how much rarer still would such complaint be, if they did not know of any different order existing anywhere else. Women do not complain of the general lot of women; or rather they do, for plaintive elegies on it are very common in the writings of women, and were still more so as long as the lamentations could not be suspected of having any practical object. Their complaints are like the complaints which men make of the general unsatisfactoriness of human life; they are not meant to imply blame, or to plead for any change. But though women do not complain of the power of husbands, each complains of her own husband, or of the husbands of her friends. It is the same in all other cases of servitude, at least in the commencement of the emancipatory movement. The serfs did not at first complain of the power of their lords, but only of their tyranny. The Commons began by claiming a few municipal privileges; they next asked an exemption for themselves from being taxed without their own consent; but they would at that time have thought it a great presumption to claim any share in the king's sovereign authority. The case of women is now the only case in which to rebel against established rules is still looked upon with the same eyes as was formerly a subject's claim to the right of rebelling against his king. A woman who joins in any movement which her husband disapproves, makes herself a martyr, without even being able to be an apostle, for the husband can legally put a stop to her apostleship. Women cannot be expected to devote themselves to the emancipation of women, until men in considerable number are prepared to join with them in the undertaking.

CHAPTER IV.

THERE remains a question, not of less importance than those already discussed, and which will be asked the most importunately by those opponents whose conviction is somewhat shaken on the main point. What good are we to expect from the changes proposed in our customs and institutions? Would mankind be at all better off if women were free? If not, why. disturb their minds, and attempt to make a social revolution in the name of an abstract right?

It is hardly to be expected that this question will be asked in respect to the change proposed in the condition of women in marriage. The sufferings, immoralities, evils of all sorts, produced in innumerable cases by the subjection of individual women to individual men, are far too terrible to be overlooked. Unthinking or uncandid persons, counting those cases alone which are extreme, or which attain publicity, may say that the evils are exceptional; but no one can be blind to their existence, nor, in many cases,

to their intensity. And it is perfectly obvious
that the abuse of the power cannot be very much
checked while the power remains. It is a power
given, or offered, not to good men, or to decently
respectable men, but to all men; the most brutal,
and the most criminal. There is no check but
that of opinion, and such men are in general
within the reach of no opinion but that of men
like themselves. If such men did not brutally
tyrannize over the one human being whom the
law compels to bear everything from them, society
must already have reached a paradisiacal state.
There could be no need any longer of laws to
curb men's vicious propensities. Astræa must
not only have returned to earth, but the heart of
the worst man must have become her temple. The
law of servitude in marriage is a monstrous contradiction to all the principles of the modern world,
and to all the experience through which those
principles have been slowly and painfully worked
out. It is the sole case, now that negro slavery has
been abolished, in which a human being in the pleni-
tude of every faculty is delivered up to the tender
mercies of another human being, in the hope
forsooth that this other will use the power solely
for the good of the person subjected to it.
Marriage is the only actual bondage known to
our law. There remain no legal slaves, except
the mistress of every house.

It is not, therefore, on this part of the subject, that the question is likely to be asked, *Cui bono ?* We may be told that the evil would outweigh the good, but the reality of the good admits of no dispute. In regard, however, to the larger question, the removal of women's disabilities— their recognition as the equals of men in all that belongs to citizenship—the opening to them of all honourable employments, and of the training and education which qualifies for those employments—there are many persons for whom it is not enough that the inequality has no just or legitimate defence; they require to be told what express advantage would be obtained by abolishing it.

To which let me first answer, the advantage of having the most universal and pervading of all human relations regulated by justice instead of injustice. The vast amount of this gain to human nature, it is hardly possible, by any explanation or illustration, to place in a stronger light than it is placed by the bare statement, to any one who attaches a moral meaning to words. All the selfish propensities, the self-worship, the unjust self-preference, which exist among mankind, have their source and root in, and derive their principal nourishment from, the present constitution of the relation between men and women. Think what it is to a boy, to grow up to manhood in the

belief that without any merit or any exertion of
his own, though he may be the most frivolous
and empty or the most ignorant and stolid of
mankind, by the mere fact of being born a male
he is by right the superior of all and every one
of an entire half of the human race : including
probably some whose real superiority to himself
he has daily or hourly occasion to feel ; but even
if in his whole conduct he habitually follows
a woman's guidance, still, if he is a fool, she
thinks that of course she is not, and cannot be,
equal in ability and judgment to himself ; and if
he is not a fool, he does worse—he sees that she
is superior to him, and believes that, notwithstanding her superiority, he is entitled to command and
she is bound to obey.   What must be the effect
on his character, of this lesson ?   And men of the
cultivated classes are often not aware how deeply
it sinks into the immense majority of male minds.
For, among right-feeling and well-bred people, the
inequality is kept as much as possible out of sight ;
above all, out of sight of the children.   As much
obedience is required from boys to their mother
as to their father : they are not permitted to
domineer over their sisters, nor are they accustomed to see these postponed to them, but the
contrary ; the compensations of the chivalrous
feeling being made prominent, while the servitude
which requires them is kept in the background.

Well brought-up youths in the higher classes
thus often escape the bad influences of the situation in their early years, and only experience them
when, arrived at manhood, they fall under the
dominion of facts as they really exist. Such
people are little aware, when a boy is differently
brought up, how early the notion of his inherent
superiority to a girl arises in his mind; how it
grows with his growth and strengthens with his
strength; how it is inoculated by one schoolboy
upon another; how early the youth thinks himself superior to his mother, owing her perhaps
forbearance, but no real respect; and how sublime
and sultan-like a sense of superiority he feels,
above all, over the woman whom he honours by
admitting her to a partnership of his life. Is it
imagined that all this does not pervert the whole
manner of existence of the man, both as an individual and as a social being? It is an exact
parallel to the feeling of a hereditary king that
he is excellent above others by being born a king,
or a noble by being born a noble. The relation
between husband and wife is very like that
between lord and vassal, except that the wife is
held to more unlimited obedience than the vassal
was. However the vassal's character may have
been affected, for better and for worse, by his
subordination, who can help seeing that the lord's
was affected greatly for the worse? whether he was

led to believe that his vassals were really superior to himself, or to feel that he was placed in command over people as good as himself, for no merits or labours of his own, but merely for having, as Figaro says, taken the trouble to be born. The self-worship of the monarch, or of the feudal superior, is matched by the self-worship of the male. Human beings do not grow up from childhood in the possession of unearned distinctions, without pluming themselves upon them. Those whom privileges not acquired by their merit, and which they feel to be disproportioned to it, inspire with additional humility, are always the few, and the best few. The rest are only inspired with pride, and the worst sort of pride, that which values itself upon accidental advantages, not of its own achieving. Above all, when the feeling of being raised above the whole of the other sex is combined with personal authority over one individual among them; the situation, if a school of conscientious and affectionate forbearance to those whose strongest points of character are conscience and affection, is to men of another quality a regularly constituted Academy or Gymnasium for training them in arrogance and overbearingness; which vices, if curbed by the certainty of resistance in their intercourse with other men, their equals, break out towards all who are in a position to be obliged to tolerate them, and often revenge themselves upon the unfortunate wife for the involuntary restraint which they are obliged to submit to elsewhere.

The example afforded, and the education given to the sentiments, by laying the foundation of domestic existence upon a relation contradictory to the first principles of social justice, must, from the very nature of man, have a perverting influence of such magnitude, that it is hardly possible with our present experience to raise our imaginations to the conception of so great a change for the better as would be made by its removal. All that education and civilization are doing to efface the influences on character of the law of force, and replace them by those of justice, remains merely on the surface, as long as the citadel of the enemy is not attacked. The principle of the modern movement in morals and politics, is that conduct, and conduct alone, entitles to respect : that not what men are, but what they do, constitutes their claim to deference; that, above all, merit, and not birth, is the only rightful claim to power and authority. If no authority, not in its nature temporary, were allowed to one human being over another, society would not be employed in building up propensities with one hand which it has to curb with the other. The child would really, for the first time in man's existence on earth, be trained in the way he should go, and when he was old there would be a chance that he would not depart from it. But so long as the right of the strong to power over the weak rules in the very heart of society, the attempt to make the equal right of the weak the principle of its outward actions will always be an uphill struggle; for the law of justice, which is also that of Christianity, will never get possession of men's inmost sentiments; they will be working against it, even when bending to it.

The second benefit to be expected from giving to women the free use of their faculties, by leaving them the free choice of their employments, and opening to them the same field of occupation and the same prizes and encouragements as to other human beings, would be that of doubling the mass of mental faculties available for the higher service of humanity. Where there is now one person qualified to benefit mankind and promote the general improvement, as a public teacher, or an administrator of some branch of public or social affairs, there would then be a chance of two. Mental superiority of any kind is at present everywhere so much below the demand; there is such a deficiency of persons competent to do excellently anything which it requires any considerable amount of ability to do; that the loss to the world, by refusing to make use of one-half of the whole quantity of talent it possesses, is

extremely serious. It is true that this amount
of mental power is not totally lost. Much of
it is employed, and would in any case be employed, in domestic management, and in the few
other occupations open to women; and from the
remainder indirect benefit is in many individual
cases obtained, through the personal influence
of individual women over individual men. But
these benefits are partial; their range is extremely
circumscribed; and if they must be admitted, on
the one hand, as a deduction from the amount
of fresh social power that would be acquired by
giving freedom to one-half of the whole sum of
human intellect, there must be added, on the
other, the benefit of the stimulus that would be
given to the intellect of men by the competition;
or (to use a more true expression) by the necessity
that would be imposed on them of deserving
precedency before they could expect to obtain it.

This great accession to the intellectual power
of the species, and to the amount of intellect
available for the good management of its affairs,
would be obtained, partly, through the better and
more complete intellectual education of women,
which would then improve *pari passu* with that
of men. Women in general would be brought up
equally capable of understanding business, public
affairs, and the higher matters of speculation, with
men in the same class of society; and the select

few of the one as well as of the other sex, who
were qualified not only to comprehend what is
done or thought by others, but to think or do
something considerable themselves, would meet
with the same facilities for improving and training
their capacities in the one sex as in the other.
In this way, the widening of the sphere of action
for women would operate for good, by raising
their education to the level of that of men, and
making the one participate in all improvements
made in the other. But independently of this,
the mere breaking down of the barrier would of
itself have an educational virtue of the highest
worth. The mere getting rid of the idea that all
the wider subjects of thought and action, all the
things which are of general and not solely of
private interest, are men's business, from which
women are to be warned off—positively interdicted
from most of it, coldly tolerated in the little
which is allowed them—the mere consciousness a
woman would then have of being a human being
like any other, entitled to choose her pursuits,
urged or invited by the same inducements as any
one else to interest herself in whatever is interesting to human beings, entitled to exert the
share of influence on all human concerns which
belongs to an individual opinion, whether she
attempted actual participation in them or not—
this alone would effect an immense expansion of

the faculties of women, as well as enlargement of the range of their moral sentiments.

Besides the addition to the amount of individual talent available for the conduct of human affairs, which certainly are not at present so abundantly provided in that respect that they can afford to dispense with one-half of what nature proffers; the opinion of women would then possess a more beneficial, rather than a greater, influence upon the general mass of human belief and sentiment. I say a more beneficial, rather than a greater influence; for the influence of women over the general tone of opinion has always, or at least from the earliest known period, been very considerable. The influence of mothers on the early character of their sons, and the desire of young men to recommend themselves to young women, have in all recorded times been important agencies in the formation of character, and have determined some of the chief steps in the progress of civilization. Even in the Homeric age, αἰδώς towards the Τρωάδας ἑλκεσιπέπλους is an acknowledged and powerful motive of action in the great Hector. The moral influence of women has had two modes of operation. First, it has been a softening influence. Those who were most liable to be the victims of violence, have naturally tended as much as they could towards limiting its sphere and mitigating its excesses. Those who were not taught to fight, have naturally inclined in favour of any other mode of settling differences rather than that of fighting. In general, those who have been the greatest sufferers by the indulgence of selfish passion, have been the most earnest supporters of any moral law which offered a means of bridling passion. Women were powerfully instrumental in inducing the northern conquerors to adopt the creed of Christianity, a creed so much more favourable to women than any that preceded it. The conversion of the Anglo-Saxons and of the Franks may be said to have been begun by the wives of Ethelbert and Clovis. The other mode in which the effect of women's opinion has been conspicuous, is by giving a powerful stimulus to those qualities in men, which, not being themselves trained in, it was necessary for them that they should find in their protectors. Courage, and the military virtues generally, have at all times been greatly indebted to the desire which men felt of being admired by women: and the stimulus reaches far beyond this one class of eminent qualities, since, by a very natural effect of their position, the best passport to the admiration and favour of women has always been to be thought highly of by men. From the combination of the two kinds of moral influence thus exercised by women, arose the spirit of chivalry : the peculiarity of which is, to aim at combining the highest standard of the warlike qualities with the cultivation of a totally different class of virtues—those of gentleness, generosity, and self-abnegation, towards the non-military and defenceless classes generally, and a special submission and worship directed towards women; who were distinguished from the other defenceless classes by the high rewards which they had it in their power voluntarily to bestow on those who endeavoured to earn their favour, instead of extorting their subjection. Though the practice of chivalry fell even more sadly short of its theoretic standard than practice generally falls below theory, it remains one of the most precious monuments of the moral history of our race ; as a remarkable instance of a concerted and organized attempt by a most disorganized and distracted society, to raise up and carry into practice a moral ideal greatly in advance of its social condition and institutions ; so much so as to have been completely frustrated in the main object, yet never entirely inefficacious, and which has left a most sensible, and for the most part a highly valuable impress on the ideas and feelings of all subsequent times.

The chivalrous ideal is the acme of the influence of women's sentiments on the moral cultivation of mankind : and if women are to remain in their subordinate situation, it were greatly to be lamented that the chivalrous standard should have passed away, for it is the only one at all capable of mitigating the demoralizing influences of that position. But the changes in the general state of the species rendered inevitable the substitution of a totally different ideal of morality for the chivalrous one. Chivalry was the attempt to infuse moral elements into a state of society in which everything depended for good or evil on individual prowess, under the softening influences of individual delicacy and generosity. In modern societies, all things, even in the military department of affairs, are decided, not by individual effort, but by the combined operations of numbers; while the main occupation of society has changed from fighting to business, from military to industrial life. The exigencies of the new life are no more exclusive of the virtues of generosity than those of the old, but it no longer entirely depends on them. The main foundations of the moral life of modern times must be justice and prudence; the respect of each for the rights of every other, and the ability of each to take care of himself. Chivalry left without legal check all forms of wrong which reigned unpunished throughout society; it only encouraged a few to do right in preference to wrong, by the direction it gave to the instruments of praise and admiration. But the real dependence of morality must always be upon its penal sanctions—its power to deter from evil. The security of society cannot rest on merely rendering honour to right, a motive so comparatively weak in all but a few, and which on very many does not operate at all. Modern society is able to repress wrong through all departments of life, by a fit exertion of the superior strength which civilization has given it, and thus to render the existence of the weaker members of society (no longer defenceless but protected by law) tolerable to them, without reliance on the chivalrous feelings of those who are in a position to tyrannize. The beauties and graces of the chivalrous character are still what they were, but the rights of the weak, and the general comfort of human life, now rest on a far surer and steadier support; or rather, they do so in every relation of life except the conjugal.

At present the moral influence of women is no less real, but it is no longer of so marked and definite a character : it has more nearly merged in the general influence of public opinion. Both through the contagion of sympathy, and through the desire of men to shine in the eyes of women, their feelings have great effect in keeping alive what remains of the chivalrous ideal—in fostering the sentiments and continuing the traditions of spirit and generosity. In these

points of character, their standard is higher than
that of men ; in the quality of justice, somewhat
lower. As regards the relations of private life
it may be said generally, that their influence is,
on the whole, encouraging to the softer virtues,
discouraging to the sterner : though the statement must be taken with all the modifications
dependent on individual character. In the
chief of the greater trials to which virtue is
subject in the concerns of life—the conflict between interest and principle—the tendency of
women's influence is of a very mixed character.
When the principle involved happens to be one
of the very few which the course of their religious or moral education has strongly impressed
upon themselves, they are potent auxiliaries to
virtue : and their husbands and sons are often
prompted by them to acts of abnegation which
they never would have been capable of without
that stimulus. But, with the present education
and position of women, the moral principles
which have been impressed on them cover but a
comparatively small part of the field of virtue,
and are, moreover, principally negative ; forbid-
ding particular acts, but having little to do with
the general direction of the thoughts and purposes. I am afraid it must be said, that disinterestedness in the general conduct of life—the
devotion of the energies to purposes which hold

out no promise of private advantages to the family—is very seldom encouraged or supported by women's influence. It is small blame to them that they discourage objects of which they have not learnt to see the advantage, and which withdraw their men from them, and from the interests of the family. But the consequence is that women's influence is often anything but favourable to public virtue.

Women have, however, some share of influence in giving the tone to public moralities since their sphere of action has been a little widened, and since a considerable number of them have occupied themselves practically in the promotion of objects reaching beyond their own family and household. The influence of women counts for a great deal in two of the most marked features of modern European life—its aversion to war, and its addiction to philanthropy. Excellent characteristics both; but unhappily, if the influence of women is valuable in the encouragement it gives to these feelings in general, in the particular applications the direction it gives to them is at least as often mischievous as useful. In the philanthropic department more particularly, the two provinces chiefly cultivated by women are religious proselytism and charity. Religious proselytism at home, is but another word for embittering of religious animosities: abroad, it is usually a

blind running at an object, without either knowing or heeding the fatal mischiefs—fatal to the
religious object itself as well as to all other
desirable objects—which may be produced by the
means employed.   As for charity, it is a matter
in which the immediate effect on the persons
directly concerned, and the ultimate consequence
to the general good, are apt to be at complete
war with one another : while the education given
to women—an education of the sentiments rather
than of the understanding—and the habit inculcated by their whole life, of looking to immediate effects on persons, and not to remote effects
on classes of persons—make them both unable
to see, and unwilling to admit, the ultimate evil
tendency of any form of charity or philanthropy
which commends itself to their sympathetic feelings. The great and continually increasing mass
of unenlightened and shortsighted benevolence,
which, taking the care of people's lives out of
their own hands, and relieving them from the
disagreeable consequences of their own acts, saps
the very foundations of the self-respect, self-help,
and self-control which are the essential conditions both of individual prosperity and of social
virtue—this waste of resources and of benevolent
feelings in doing harm instead of good, is immensely swelled by women's contributions, and
stimulated by their influence.   Not that this is

a mistake likely to be made by women, where they have actually the practical management of schemes of beneficence. It sometimes happens that women who administer public charities—with that insight into present fact, and especially into the minds and feelings of those with whom they are in immediate contact, in which women generally excel men—recognise in the clearest manner the demoralizing influence of the alms given or the help afforded, and could give lessons on the subject to many a male political economist. But women who only give their money, and are not brought face to face with the effects it produces, how can they be expected to foresee them? A woman born to the present lot of women, and content with it, how should she appreciate the value of self-dependence? She is not self-dependent; she is not taught self-dependence; her destiny is to receive everything from others, and why should what is good enough for her be bad for the poor? Her familiar notions of good are of blessings descending from a superior. She forgets that she is not free, and that the poor are; that if what they need is given to them unearned, they cannot be compelled to earn it: that everybody cannot be taken care of by everybody, but there must be some motive to induce people to take care of themselves; and that to be helped to help themselves, if they are physically capable of it, is the only charity which proves to be charity in the end.

These considerations shew how usefully the part which women take in the formation of general opinion, would be modified for the better by that more enlarged instruction, and practical conversancy with the things which their opinions influence, that would necessarily arise from their social and political emancipation. But the improvement it would work through the influence they exercise, each in her own family, would be still more remarkable.

It is often said that in the classes most exposed to temptation, a man's wife and children tend to keep him honest and respectable, both by the wife's direct influence, and by the concern he feels for their future welfare. This may be so, and no doubt often is so, with those who are more weak than wicked; and this beneficial influence would be preserved and strengthened under equal laws; it does not depend on the woman's servitude, but is, on the contrary, diminished by the disrespect which the inferior class of men always at heart feel towards those who are subject to their power. But when we ascend higher in the scale, we come among a totally different set of moving forces. The wife's influence tends, as far as it goes, to prevent the husband from falling below the common standard

of approbation of the country. It tends quite as
strongly to hinder him from rising above it.
The wife is the auxiliary of the common public
opinion. A man who is married to a woman
his inferior in intelligence, finds her a perpetual
dead weight, or, worse than a dead weight, a
drag, upon every aspiration of his to be better
than public opinion requires him to be. It is
hardly possible for one who is in these bonds, to
attain exalted virtue. If he differs in his opinion
from the mass—if he sees truths which have not
yet dawned upon them, or if, feeling in his heart
truths which they nominally recognise, he would
like to act up to those truths more conscien-
tiously than the generality of mankind—to all
such thoughts and desires, marriage is the heaviest
of drawbacks, unless he be so fortunate as to
have a wife as much above the common level as
he himself is.

For, in the first place, there is always some
sacrifice of personal interest required ; either of
social consequence, or of pecuniary means; perhaps the risk of even the means of subsistence.
These sacrifices and risks he may be willing to
encounter for himself; but he will pause before
he imposes them on his family. And his family
in this case means his wife and daughters; for
he always hopes that his sons will feel as he feels
himself, and that what he can do without, they

will do without, willingly, in the same cause. But his daughters—their marriage may depend upon it: and his wife, who is unable to enter into or understand the objects for which these sacrifices are made—who, if she thought them worth any sacrifice, would think so on trust, and solely for his sake—who can participate in none of the enthusiasm or the self-approbation he himself may feel, while the things which he is disposed to sacrifice are all in all to her; will not the best and most unselfish man hesitate the longest before bringing on her this consequence? If it be not the comforts of life, but only social consideration, that is at stake, the burthen upon his conscience and feelings is still very severe. Whoever has a wife and children has given hostages to Mrs. Grundy. The approbation of that potentate may be a matter of indifference to him, but it is of great importance to his wife. The man himself may be above opinion, or may find sufficient compensation in the opinion of those of his own way of thinking. But to the women connected with him, he can offer no compensation. The almost invariable tendency of the wife to place her influence in the same scale with social consideration, is sometimes made a reproach to women, and represented as a peculiar trait of feebleness and childishness of character in them: surely with great injustice.

Society makes the whole life of a woman, in the easy classes, a continued self-sacrifice; it exacts from her an unremitting restraint of the whole of her natural inclinations, and the sole return it makes to her for what often deserves the name of a martyrdom, is consideration. Her consideration is inseparably connected with that of her husband, and after paying the full price for it, she finds that she is to lose it, for no reason of which she can feel the cogency. She has sacrificed her whole life to it, and her husband will not sacrifice to it a whim, a freak, an eccentricity; something not recognised or allowed for by the world, and which the world will agree with her in thinking a folly, if it thinks no worse! The dilemma is hardest upon that very meritorious class of men, who, without possessing talents which qualify them to make a figure among those with whom they agree in opinion, hold their opinion from conviction, and feel bound in honour and conscience to serve it, by making profession of their belief, and giving their time, labour, and means, to anything undertaken in its behalf. The worst case of all is when such men happen to be of a rank and position which of itself neither gives them, nor excludes them from, what is considered the best society; when their admission to it depends mainly on what is thought of them personally—and however unexceptionable their breeding and habits, their being identified with opinions and public conduct unacceptable to those who give the tone to society would operate as an effectual exclusion. Many a woman flatters herself (nine times out of ten quite erroneously) that nothing prevents her and her husband from moving in the highest society of her neighbourhood—society in which others well known to her, and in the same class of life, mix freely—except that her husband is unfortunately a Dissenter, or has the reputation of mingling in low radical politics. That it is, she thinks, which hinders George from getting a commission or a place, Caroline from making an advantageous match, and prevents her and her husband from obtaining invitations, perhaps honours, which, for aught she sees, they are as well entitled to as some folks. With such an influence in every house, either exerted actively, or operating all the more powerfully for not being asserted, is it any wonder that people in general are kept down in that mediocrity of respectability which is becoming a marked characteristic of modern times ?

There is another very injurious aspect in which the effect, not of women's disabilities directly, but of the broad line of difference which those disabilities create between the education and character of a woman and that of a man, requires to

be considered. Nothing can be more unfavourable to that union of thoughts and inclinations
which is the ideal of married life. Intimate
society between people radically dissimilar to one
another, is an idle dream. Unlikeness may attract,
but it is likeness which retains ; and in proportion
to the likeness is the suitability of the individuals
to give each other a happy life. While women
are so unlike men, it is not wonderful that selfish
men should feel the need of arbitrary power in
their own hands, to arrest *in limine* the life-long
conflict of inclinations, by deciding every question
on the side of their own preference. When people
are extremely unlike, there can be no real identity
of interest. Very often there is conscientious
difference of opinion between married people, on
the highest points of duty. Is there any reality
in the marriage union where this takes place?
Yet it is not uncommon anywhere, when the
woman has any earnestness of character ; and it
is a very general case indeed in Catholic countries,
when she is supported in her dissent by the only
other authority to which she is taught to bow, the
priest. With the usual barefacedness of power
not accustomed to find itself disputed, the influence of priests over women is attacked by Pro-
testant and Liberal writers, less for being bad in
itself, than because it is a rival authority to the
husband, and raises up a revolt against his infal-

libility. In England, similar differences occasionally exist when an Evangelical wife has allied herself with a husband of a different quality ; but in general this source at least of dissension is got rid of, by reducing the minds of women to such a nullity, that they have no opinions but those of Mrs. Grundy, or those which the husband tells them to have. When there is no difference of opinion, differences merely of taste may be sufficient to detract greatly from the happiness of married life. And though it may stimulate the amatory propensities of men, it does not conduce to married happiness, to exaggerate by differences of education whatever may be the native differences of the sexes. If the married pair are well-bred and well-behaved people, they tolerate each other's tastes ; but is mutual toleration what people look forward to, when they enter into marriage ? These differences of inclination will naturally make their wishes different, if not restrained by affection or duty, as to almost all domestic questions which arise. What a difference there must be in the society which the two persons will wish to frequent, or be frequented by ! Each will desire associates who share their own tastes : the persons agreeable to one, will be indifferent or positively disagreeable to the other ; yet there can be none who are not common to both, for married people do not now live in dif-

ferent parts of the house and have totally different visiting lists, as in the reign of Louis XV.
They cannot help having different wishes as to
the bringing up of the children : each will wish to
see reproduced in them their own tastes and sentiments : and there is either a compromise, and only
a half-satisfaction to either, or the wife has to
yield—often with bitter suffering ; and, with or
without intention, her occult influence continues
to counterwork the husband's purposes.

It would of course be extreme folly to suppose
that these differences of feeling and inclination
only exist because women are brought up differently from men, and that there would not be
differences of taste under any imaginable circumstances. But there is nothing beyond the mark
in saying that the distinction in bringing-up
immensely aggravates those differences, and
renders them wholly inevitable. While women
are brought up as they are, a man and a woman
will but rarely find in one another real agreement of tastes and wishes as to daily life. They
will generally have to give it up as hopeless, and
renounce the attempt to have, in the intimate
associate of their daily life, that *idem velle, idem
nolle,* which is the recognised bond of any society
that is really such : or if the man succeeds in
obtaining it, he does so by choosing a woman
who is so complete a nullity that she has no

velle or *nolle* at all, and is as ready to comply with one thing as another if anybody tells her to do so. Even this calculation is apt to fail; dulness and want of spirit are not always a guarantee of the submission which is so confidently expected from them. But if they were, is this the ideal of marriage? What, in this case, does the man obtain by it, except an upper servant, a nurse, or a mistress? On the contrary, when each of two persons, instead of being a nothing, is a something; when they are attached to one another, and are not too much unlike to begin with; the constant partaking in the same things, assisted by their sympathy, draws out the latent capacities of each for being interested in the things which were at first interesting only to the other; and works a gradual assimilation of the tastes and characters to one another, partly by the insensible modification of each, but more by a real enriching of the two natures, each acquiring the tastes and capacities of the other in addition to its own. This often happens between two friends of the same sex, who are much associated in their daily life : and it would be a common, if not the commonest, case in marriage, did not the totally different bringing-up of the two sexes make it next to an impossibility to form a really well-assorted union. Were this remedied, whatever differences there might still be in individual tastes, there would at least be, as a general rule, complete unity and unanimity as to the great objects of life. When the two persons both care for great objects, and are a help and encouragement to each other in whatever regards these, the minor matters on which their tastes may differ are not all-important to them; and there is a foundation for solid friendship, of an enduring character, more likely than anything else to make it, through the whole of life, a greater pleasure to each to give pleasure to the other, than to receive it.

I have considered, thus far, the effects on the pleasures and benefits of the marriage union which depend on the mere unlikeness between the wife and the husband : but the evil tendency is prodigiously aggravated when the unlikeness is inferiority. Mere unlikeness, when it only means difference of good qualities, may be more a benefit in the way of mutual improvement, than a drawback from comfort. When each emulates, and desires and endeavours to acquire, the other's peculiar qualities, the difference does not produce diversity of interest, but increased identity of it, and makes each still more valuable to the other. But when one is much the inferior of the two in mental ability and cultivation, and is not actively attempting by the other's aid to rise to the other's level, the whole influence of the connexion upon

the development of the superior of the two is
deteriorating : and still more so in a tolerably
happy marriage than in an unhappy one.   It is
not with impunity that the superior in intellect
shuts himself up with an inferior, and elects
that inferior for his chosen, and sole completely
intimate, associate.   Any society which is not improving, is deteriorating : and the more so, the
closer and more familiar it is.   Even a really
superior man almost always begins to deteriorate
when he is habitually (as the phrase is) king of his
company : and in his most habitual company the
husband who has a wife inferior to him is always so.
While his self-satisfaction is incessantly ministered
to on the one hand, on the other he insensibly
imbibes the modes of feeling, and of looking at
things, which belong to a more vulgar or a more
limited mind than his own.   This evil differs
from many of those which have hitherto been
dwelt on, by being an increasing one.   The
association of men with women in daily life is
much closer and more complete than it ever was
before.   Men's life is more domestic.   Formerly,
their pleasures and chosen occupations were
among men, and in men's company : their wives
had but a fragment of their lives.   At the present
time, the progress of civilization, and the turn of
opinion against the rough amusements and con-
vivial excesses which formerly occupied most men

in their hours of relaxation—together with (it must be said) the improved tone of modern feeling as to the reciprocity of duty which binds the husband towards the wife—have thrown the man very much more upon home and its inmates, for his personal and social pleasures : while the kind and degree of improvement which has been made in women's education, has made them in some degree capable of being his companions in ideas and mental tastes, while leaving them, in most cases, still hopelessly inferior to him. His desire of mental communion is thus in general satisfied by a communion from which he learns nothing. An unimproving and unstimulating companionship is substituted for (what he might otherwise have been obliged to seek) the society of his equals in powers and his fellows in the higher pursuits. We see, accordingly, that young men of the greatest promise generally cease to improve as soon as they marry, and, not improving, inevitably degenerate. If the wife does not push the husband forward, she always holds him back. He ceases to care for what she does not care for ; he no longer desires, and ends by disliking and shunning, society congenial to his former aspirations, and which would now shame his falling-off from them ; his higher faculties both of mind and heart cease to be called into activity. And this change coinciding with the new and

selfish interests which are created by the family,
after a few years he differs in no material respect
from those who have never had wishes for anything but the common vanities and the common
pecuniary objects.

What marriage may be in the case of two
persons of cultivated faculties, identical in opinions and purposes, between whom there exists
that best kind of equality, similarity of powers
and capacities with reciprocal superiority in them
—so that each can enjoy the luxury of looking up
to the other, and can have alternately the pleasure
of leading and of being led in the path of development—I will not attempt to describe.   To those
who can conceive it, there is no need ; to those
who cannot, it would appear the dream of an
enthusiast.   But I maintain, with the profoundest
conviction, that this, and this only, is the ideal of
marriage ; and that all opinions, customs, and institutions which favour any other notion of it, or
turn the conceptions and aspirations connected
with it into any other direction, by whatever pre-
tences they may be coloured, are relics of primitive
barbarism.   The moral regeneration of mankind
will only really commence, when the most fundamental of the social relations is placed under the
rule of equal justice, and when human beings
learn to cultivate their strongest sympathy with
an equal in rights and in cultivation.

Thus far, the benefits which it has appeared that the world would gain by ceasing to make sex a disqualification for privileges and a badge of subjection, are social rather than individual; consisting in an increase of the general fund of thinking and acting power, and an improvement in the general conditions of the association of men with women. But it would be a grievous understatement of the case to omit the most direct benefit of all, the unspeakable gain in private happiness to the liberated half of the species; the difference to them between a life of subjection to the will of others, and a life of rational freedom. After the primary necessities of food and raiment, freedom is the first and strongest want of human nature. While mankind are lawless, their desire is for lawless freedom. When they have learnt to understand the meaning of duty and the value of reason, they incline more and more to be guided and restrained by these in the exercise of their freedom; but they do not therefore desire freedom less; they do not become disposed to accept the will of other people as the representative and interpreter of those guiding principles. On the contrary, the communities in which the reason has been most cultivated, and in which the idea of social duty has been most powerful, are those which have most strongly asserted the freedom of action of the individual—the liberty of each to govern his conduct by his own feelings of duty, and by such laws and social restraints as his own conscience can subscribe to.

He who would rightly appreciate the worth of personal independence as an element of happiness, should consider the value he himself puts upon it as an ingredient of his own. There is no subject on which there is a greater habitual difference of judgment between a man judging for himself, and the same man judging for other people. When he hears others complaining that they are not allowed freedom of action—that their own will has not sufficient influence in the regulation of their affairs—his inclination is, to ask, what are their grievances? what positive damage they sustain? and in what respect they consider their affairs to be mismanaged? and if they fail to make out, in answer to these questions, what appears to him a sufficient case, he turns a deaf ear, and regards their complaint as the fanciful querulousness of people whom nothing reasonable will satisfy. But he has a quite different standard of judgment when he is deciding for himself. Then, the most unexceptionable administration of his interests by a tutor set over him, does not satisfy his feelings : his personal exclusion from the deciding authority appears itself the greatest grievance of all, rendering it superfluous even to

enter into the question of mismanagement. It is
the same with nations. What citizen of a free
country would listen to any offers of good and
skilful administration, in return for the abdica-
tion of freedom? Even if he could believe that
good and skilful administration can exist among
a people ruled by a will not their own, would
not the consciousness of working out their
own destiny under their own moral responsibility be a compensation to his feelings for
great rudeness and imperfection in the details of
public affairs? Let him rest assured that whatever he feels on this point, women feel in a fully
equal degree. Whatever has been said or written,
from the time of Herodotus to the present, of the
ennobling influence of free government—the nerve
and spring which it gives to all the faculties, the
larger and higher objects which it presents to the
intellect and feelings, the more unselfish public
spirit, and calmer and broader views of duty,
that it engenders, and the generally loftier plat-
form on which it elevates the individual as, a moral,
spiritual, and social being — is every particle
as true of women as of men. Are these things
no important part of individual happiness? Let
any man call to mind what he himself felt on
emerging from boyhood—from the tutelage and
control of even loved and affectionate elders—and
entering upon the responsibilities of manhood.

Was it not like the physical effect of taking off a
heavy weight, or releasing him from obstructive,
even if not otherwise painful, bonds ? Did he
not feel twice as much alive, twice as much a
human being, as before ? And does he imagine
that women have none of these feelings ? But it
is a striking fact, that the satisfactions and
mortifications of personal pride, though all in all
to most men when the case is their own, have
less allowance made for them in the case of other
people, and are less listened to as a ground or a
justification of conduct, than any other natural
human feelings ; perhaps because men compliment
them in their own case with the names of so
many other qualities, that they are seldom
conscious how mighty an influence these feelings
exercise in their own lives. No less large and
powerful is their part, we may assure ourselves, in
the lives and feelings of women. Women are
schooled into suppressing them in their most
natural and most healthy direction, but the internal principle remains, in a different outward
form. An active and energetic mind, if denied
liberty, will seek for power : refused the command of itself, it will assert its personality by
attempting to control others. To allow to any
human beings no existence of their own but
what depends on others, is giving far too
high a premium on bending others to their pur-

poses. Where liberty cannot be hoped for, and power can, power becomes the grand object of human desire ; those to whom others will not leave the undisturbed management of their own affairs, will compensate themselves, if they can, by meddling for their own purposes with the affairs of others. Hence also women's passion for personal beauty, and dress and display ; and all the evils that flow from it, in the way of mischievous luxury and social immorality. The love of power and the love of liberty are in eternal antagonism. Where there is least liberty, the passion for power is the most ardent and unscrupulous. The desire of power over others can only cease to be a depraving agency among mankind, when each of them individually is able to do without it : which can only be where respect for liberty in the personal concerns of each is an established principle.

But it is not only through the sentiment of personal dignity, that the free direction and disposal of their own faculties is a source of individual happiness, and to be fettered and restricted in it, a source of unhappiness, to human beings, and not least to women. There is nothing, after disease, indigence, and guilt, so fatal to the pleasurable enjoyment of life as the want of a worthy outlet for the active faculties. Women who have the cares of a family, and while they have the cares of a family, have this outlet, and it generally

suffices for them : but what of the greatly increasing number of women, who have had no
opportunity of exercising the vocation which
they are mocked by telling them is their proper
one ? What of the women whose children have
been lost to them by death or distance, or have
grown up, married, and formed homes of their
own? There are abundant examples of men
who, after a life engrossed by business, retire with
a competency to the enjoyment, as they hope, of
rest, but to whom, as they are unable to acquire
new interests and excitements that can replace
the old, the change to a life of inactivity brings
ennui, melancholy, and premature death. Yet
no one thinks of the parallel case of so many
worthy and devoted women, who, having paid what
they are told is their debt to society—having
brought up a family blamelessly to manhood and
womanhood—having kept a house as long as they
had a house needing to be kept—are deserted by
the sole occupation for which they have fitted
themselves ; and remain with undiminished activity
but with no employment for it, unless perhaps a
daughter or daughter-in-law is willing to abdicate
in their favour the discharge of the same functions in her younger household. Surely a hard
lot for the old age of those who have worthily
discharged, as long as it was given to them to
discharge, what the world accounts their only

social duty. Of such women, and of those others
to whom this duty has not been committed at
all—many of whom pine through life with the
consciousness of thwarted vocations, and activities which are not suffered to expand—the
only resources, speaking generally, are religion
and charity. But their religion, though it may
be one of feeling, and of ceremonial observance,
cannot be a religion of action, unless in the
form of charity. For charity many of them are
by nature admirably fitted ; but to practise it
usefully, or even without doing mischief, requires
the education, the manifold preparation, the knowledge and the thinking powers, of a skilful administrator. There are few of the administrative
functions of government for which a person would
not be fit, who is fit to bestow charity usefully.
In this as in other cases (pre-eminently in that
of the education of children), the duties permitted to women cannot be performed properly,
without their being trained for duties which, to
the great loss of society, are not permitted to
them. And here let me notice the singular way
in which the question of women's disabilities is
frequently presented to view, by those who find
it easier to draw a ludicrous picture of what they
do not like, than to answer the arguments for it.
When it is suggested that women's executive
capacities and prudent counsels might sometimes

be found valuable in affairs of state, these lovers of fun hold up to the ridicule of the world, as sitting in parliament or in the cabinet, girls in their teens, or young wives of two or three and twenty, transported bodily, exactly as they are, from the drawing-room to the House of Commons. They forget that males are not usually selected at this early age for a seat in Parliament, or for responsible political functions. Common sense would tell them that if such trusts were confided to women, it would be to such as having no special vocation for married life, or preferring another employment of their faculties (as many women even now prefer to marriage some of the few honourable occupations within their reach), have spent the best years of their youth in attempting to qualify themselves for the pursuits in which they desire to engage; or still more frequently perhaps, widows or wives of forty or fifty, by whom the knowledge of life and faculty of government which they have acquired in their families, could by the aid of appropriate studies be made available on a less contracted scale. There is no country of Europe in which the ablest men have not frequently experienced, and keenly appreciated, the value of the advice and help of clever and experienced women of the world, in the attainment both of private and of public objects; and there are important matters of public administration to which few men are equally competent with such women ; among others, the detailed control of expenditure. But what we are now discussing is not the need which society has of the services of women in public business, but the dull and hopeless life to which it so often condemns them, by forbidding-them to exercise the practical abilities which many of them are conscious of, in any wider field than one which to some of them never was, and to others is no longer, open. If there is anything vitally important to the happiness of human beings, it is that they should relish their habitual pursuit. This requisite of an enjoyable life is very imperfectly granted, or altogether denied, to a large part of mankind ; and by its absence many a life is a failure, which is provided, in appearance, with every requisite of success. But if circumstances which society is not yet skilful enough to overcome, render such failures often for the present inevitable, society need not itself inflict them. The injudiciousness of parents, a youth's own inexperience, or the absence of external opportunities for the congenial vocation, and their presence for an uncongenial, condemn numbers of men to pass their lives in doing one thing reluctantly and ill, when there are other things which they could have done well and happily. But on women this sentence is imposed by actual law, and by customs equivalent to law. What, in unenlightened societies, colour, race, religion, or in the case of a conquered country, nationality, are to some men, sex is to all women; a peremptory exclusion from almost all honourable occupations, but either such as cannot be fulfilled by others, or such as those others do not think worthy of their acceptance. Sufferings arising from causes of this nature usually meet with so little sympathy, that few persons are aware of the great amount of unhappiness even now produced by the feeling of a wasted life. The case will be even more frequent, as increased cultivation creates a greater and greater disproportion between the ideas and faculties of women, and the scope which society allows to their activity.

When we consider the positive evil caused to the disqualified half of the human race by their disqualification—first in the loss of the most inspiriting and elevating kind of personal enjoyment, and next in the weariness, disappointment, and profound dissatisfaction with life, which are so often the substitute for it; one feels that among all the lessons which men require for carrying on the struggle against the inevitable imperfections of their lot on earth, there is no lesson which they more need, than not to add to the evils which nature inflicts, by their jealous and prejudiced restrictions on one another. Their vain fears only substitute other and worse evils for those which they are idly apprehensive of: while every restraint on the freedom of conduct of any of their human fellow creatures, (otherwise than by making them responsible for any evil actually caused by it), dries up *pro tanto* the principal fountain of human happiness, and leaves the species less rich, to an inappreciable degree, in all that makes life valuable to the individual human being.

THE END.